AF256136

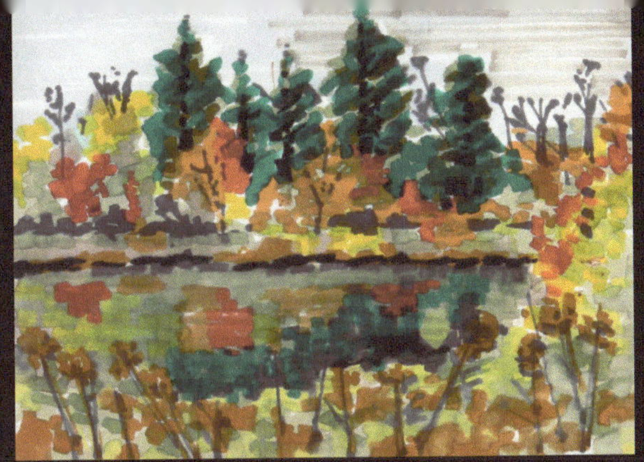

Sketch While You Travel

Richard Gerstman

Also by the author:

Branding @ the digital age by Herb Meyers and Richard Gerstman, Palgrave Macmillan

The Visionary Package by Herb Meyers and Richard Gerstman, Palgrave Macmillan

Creativity – Unconventional Wisdom from 20 Accomplished Minds by Herb Meyers and Richard Gerstman, Palgrave Macmillan

Business Ours by Herb Meyers and Richard Gerstman, Tate Publishing & Enterprises

Scandinavia in 1962 by Richard Gerstman, Blurb Books

Dedicated to my loving wife Jo Ann, daughter Kim and son Bruce, who when traveling with me always encourage and appreciate my artwork.

Contents

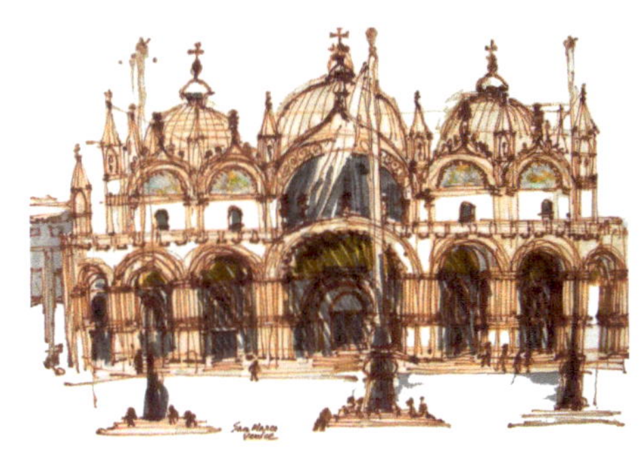

Introduction

If you like to sketch and if you like to travel, your traveling can take on a whole new dimension. This book is written to inform you about the fun of seeing new places along with making drawings that will always bring you memories of the places you visited. Your interest in travel may change from not only seeing these new places but also in relaxing and making sketches of scenes and structures that you think are appealing.

We all like to take photos while we travel and the photos sometimes become part of our memories for the future. But spending the time to sketch is different from taking camera shots, since sketching requires concentration on the architectural and botanical elements, reproducing your favorite elements in their color, light, and shadows. These elements may actually change while you are sketching them, and it becomes a challenge to make this art.

But once you make the drawing, you have something that you can save forever and you'll remember those details much better than if you had photographed it. You will be able to sketch the shape of the items, the individual colors, the botanical and natural elements, the unique architectural elements, and all the pieces that go into the scene that you are drawing.

I have traveled to many parts of the world and wherever I travel I bring my sketchbook practically each day. I look for a place that provides for me an interesting object to draw, and it is worth spending that hour or two that it takes for me to make the drawing.

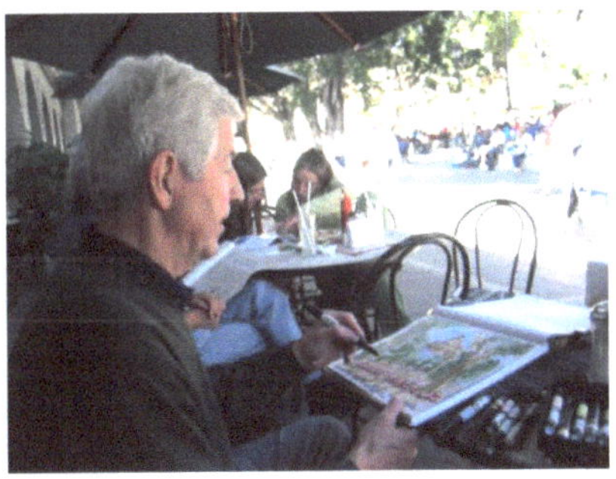

This book explains how you can sketch efficiently and still have the time to discover and tour many new locations.

After reading this book, I think you will be enthusiastic about sketching the places that you visit. You may prefer a very quick sketch taking only a few minutes, or a more detailed drawing taking a few hours. You do not have to be a great artist to take part in this activity. Whatever drawings you make will be wonderful memories for you in the future, especially since you will probably remember the specific details of what you saw, where you were when you saw it, and what the circumstances there were at the time you made the drawing.

You can use any medium for your art. For example, you may prefer watercolors, or colored pencils, or markers. I personally prefer markers on a slightly absorbent paper because of the portability of the markers and the drawing pad and their ease-of-use under most conditions. I also use an iPad with an app called "Brushes Redux". The iPad gives me the most portability while traveling, since I do not have to also carry the larger sketchbook and color markers to accommodate it. The explanations and sketches in this book are made from my drawing pad (with markers) and my iPad (with stylus). So sketch using whatever medium you like.

I do hope that this book encourages you to give your artwork a try. And see if you feel as I do – that the sketching part of the trip adds excitement and interest to your traveling experience.

Getting Started

THE MATERIALS

There is always a bit of apprehension when you prepare for a trip, especially a trip overseas. You know you're going to have to bring certain items or equipment for overseas travel and you can probably find these items near home, but not find them as easily while you are traveling.

It is important that you carry materials that are portable and easy to handle. This includes a drawing pad, which should be a size that's comfortable to carry and a size that you enjoy working on. I personally prefer an 11 x 14 pad with slightly absorbent paper so that the sketching and the color flow freely on the paper while I'm working. A sheet of paper inserted under the drawing paper layer keeps the colors from bleeding through. It's fine to bring a small pad if you like to work smaller, but I recommend not bringing a very large drawing pad, since the portability becomes a problem when traveling in many locations.

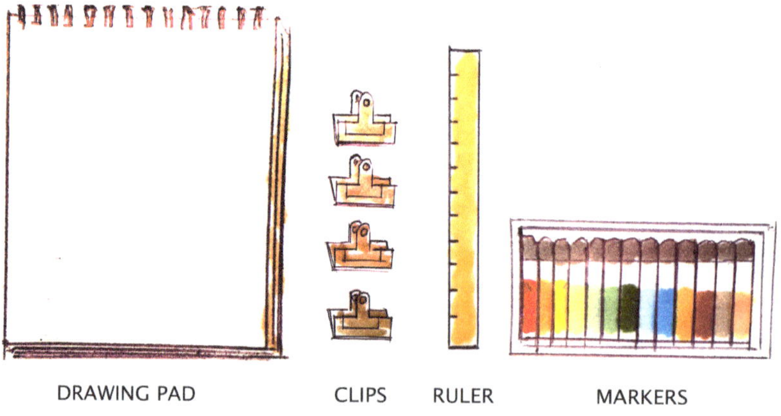

The next items are your drawing instruments. I prefer the portability of markers, since they are designed for their ease of use indoors and outdoors, come in a wide variety of colors, and require no color mixing or clean-up.

Watercolors will work in a similar fashion to markers and you may be inclined to like to work with them, but they do require more setting up at your travel site along with the extra cleanup required. While traveling, I find that it is important to move quickly when I am drawing, and therefore I prefer using markers.

You should also limit your colors to what you will actually need, and be careful not to bring too many of the markers since they take up space, and add to the weight of what you are carrying. Purchase a small plastic box in which you can put the markers. On the following page I have recommendations of colors that I have found best and most useful for travel through my many years of drawing and traveling experience.

The next essential item is a knapsack. Bring a small lightweight knapsack that can accommodate your drawing pad, markers, and a few other items.

The next item is optional, but it is handy on some occasions. It is the small, folding easel. There are lightweight easels that can be folded down to the size of a folded umbrella, and these can fit in your knapsack. I carry the easel only some of the time, and there have been occasions where the easel has been useful when I can't find other places on which to lean my drawing pad.

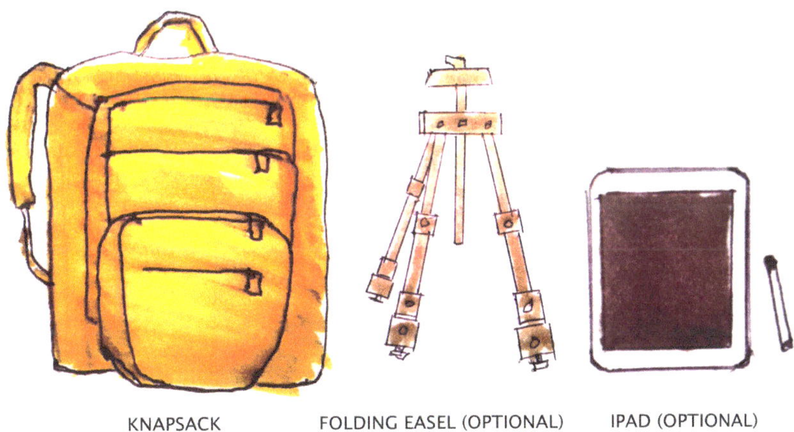

KNAPSACK   FOLDING EASEL (OPTIONAL)   IPAD (OPTIONAL)

Your materials should include four clips to hold loose paper to your pad, and a straightedge or ruler. I prefer drawing all my lines freehand, but the straightedge or ruler can help to make a determination of angles and proportions.

TRAVELING COLORS

As mentioned previously, for traveling you should bring only those colors that you will need. This will allow you to work more quickly and carry less weight, both important elements of sketching while you travel.

There are 20 marker colors that I have found through experience can work in almost every situation. This includes the following colors:

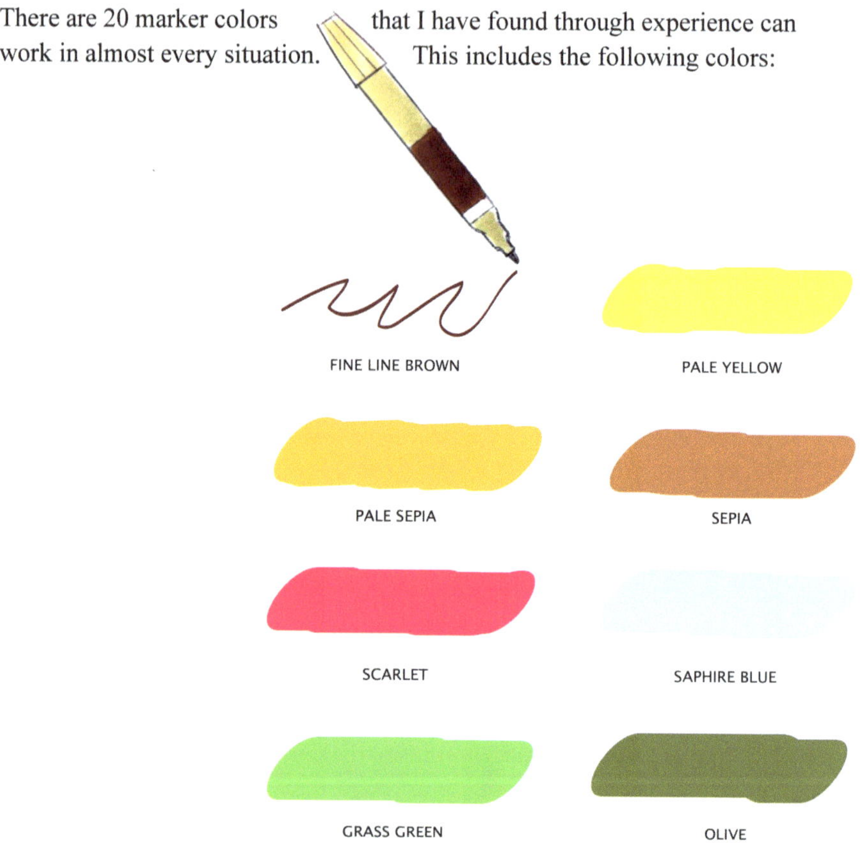

A different marker is used for each of these colors and the markers should have flat nibs on each for filling in the colors on your drawings. My recommendation is to also bring a couple of fine point markers – either in gray, brown, or black. This is the marker you will use for the original line work of your drawing, unless you prefer using a pencil. Whichever color you decide to use for your fine marker, bring an extra one, since it's important that the fine point markers not run out of ink.

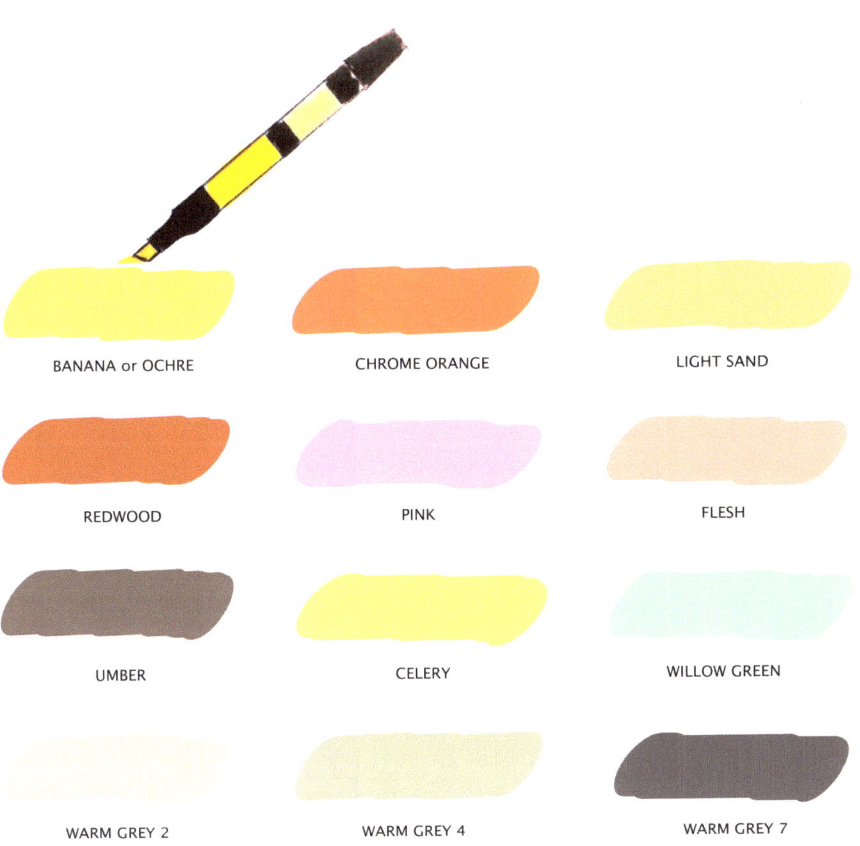

The rest of the drawing can be handled quickly and efficiently with the flat nib markers. Flat nib markers can also make a thin line by using the corner of the nib; a medium line by using the end of the nib; and a wide line by using the wide side of the nib. There are many brands of markers and most work well. I prefer the AD Markers since the inks flow well and the markers do not dry up quickly. Keep your tops tight on the markers and store them away from sunlight and they will last even for years. They can be purchased at art stores or on the internet.

ON THE ROAD

Once you find the site that you would like to draw, you need to set up your materials so that you can confidently and conveniently make your drawing. As part of traveling, most of your drawings will probably be made outdoors, and setting up an easel is not often a convenient method, especially when you don't have a hard surface under you. As part of my setting up, I look for something on which to rest the drawing pad and the markers as well.

Many of my drawings have been done while leaning on a fence, a stone wall, a rock, some steps, or even a trashcan. Sometimes you are fortunate enough to find a table on which to rest your pad and even a chair on which to sit. Take the time to comfortably set up your pad and materials, so that you can work on your drawing confidently and efficiently. I have moved large trashcans from one place to the other in order to get the best spot for drawing. This is especially true when I don't have my folding easel with me or when the conditions don't allow for a standing easel.

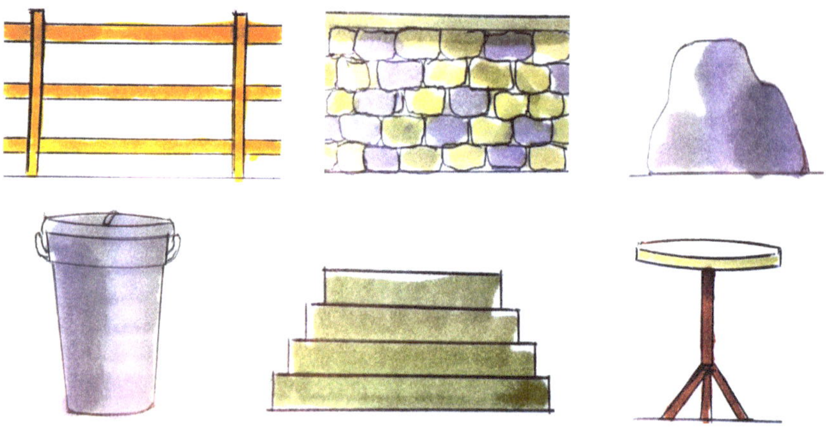

If you are unable to find a leaning surface, you can resort to sitting on the ground. This photo shows me drawing from my ground view recently in Hanoi, Vietnam, with curious onlookers.

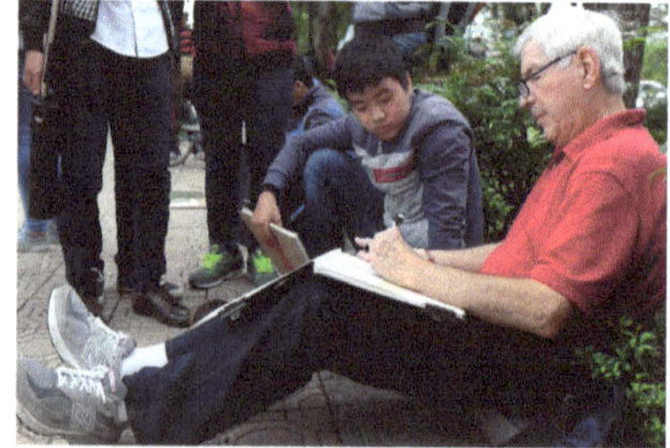

Perspective Drawing

During your travels you have found the subject -- scene, structure, building, boat, statue -- that you want to sketch. You are now standing or sitting in front of this subject and it is time to start sketching.

Perspective drawing creates the illusion of a three-dimensional space on your two dimensional piece of paper. I have found that many of my outdoor drawings use the 2-point perspective, whereas many indoor or confined area drawings use the 1-point perspective. Overall, for traveling you will probably find the 2-point perspective most useful.

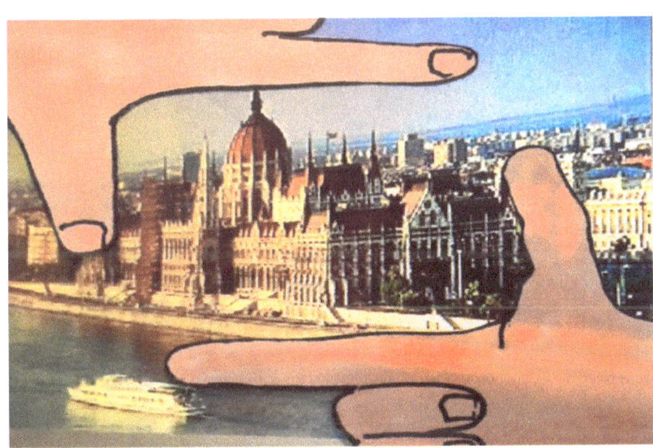

The first step in making the artwork is to frame out what you would like to see on your paper. By forming a rectangle with your hands and moving your hands to the size that surrounds the subject that you would like to see on your paper, you have made your first determination for the artwork.

Most of the things that you draw during your travels will require the framing out of the perspective. With experience, determining the perspective and its proportions will come more easily. I'll explain the steps that I take to accomplish the perspective, while keeping the process as simple as possible.

2-POINT PERSPECTIVE

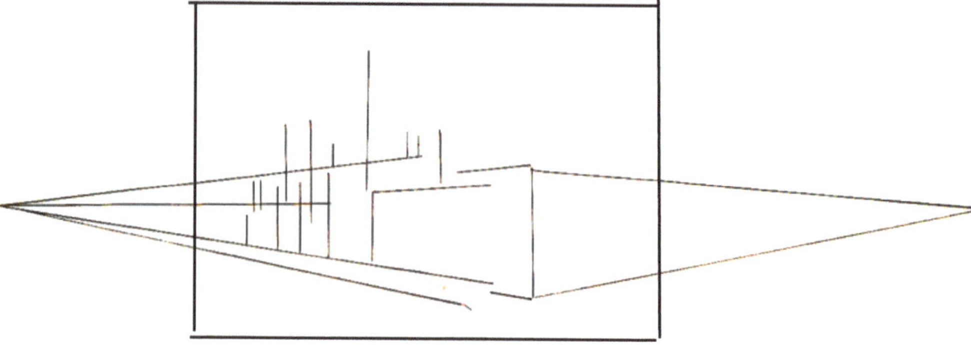

From the view of the subject that you have selected, make small points on your drawing paper to show the highest point that your subject will appear, the lowest point that your subject will appear and the side points of the subject you wish to appear on your drawing.

Use your straightedge or ruler and determine the horizontal angles from the subject that will make up your drawing. These angles will lead you to an imaginary vanishing point on the left and an imaginary vanishing point on the right. These vanishing points will probably not fit on your drawing pad. But you should keep in your mind that the angles that you have determined to use in your drawing would eventually end up at those vanishing points. All the horizontal lines in your drawing will be based on angles that eventually reach each of these imaginary vanishing points.

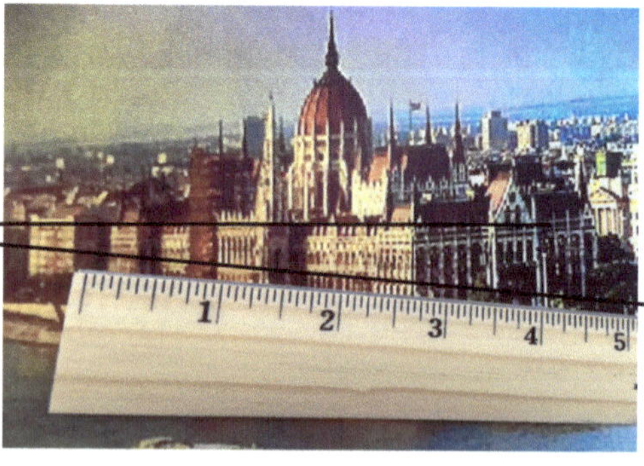

Use your straightedge or ruler to determine the proportional distances on your drawing paper from one part of the subject to the next part of the subject This includes the horizontal and vertical distances from one item on your drawing to the next item on your drawing. Make lines on your paper to represent those distances and represent the items.

2-POINT PERSPECTIVE

The next step is to start adding and connecting more lines and curves to the lines that you made on your paper. The elements of your drawing are now starting to take shape into specific structural elements.

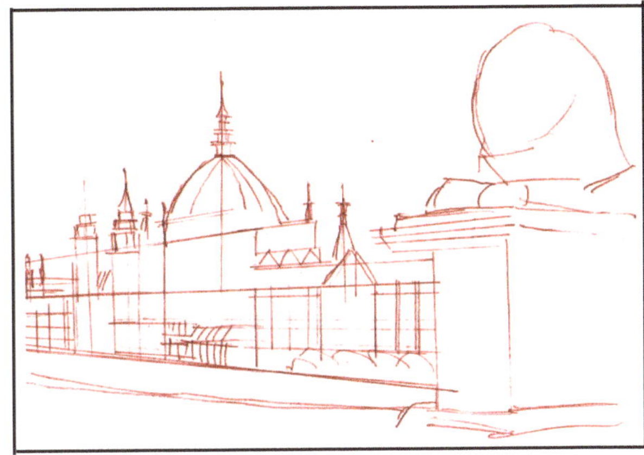

With your pencil or fine marker, add details such as windows, doors, steeples or any items that make up the elements for your drawing. Your sketch has now been laid out in line work. If you feel the layout and the proportions of the elements work well, it is now time to add the layer of color.

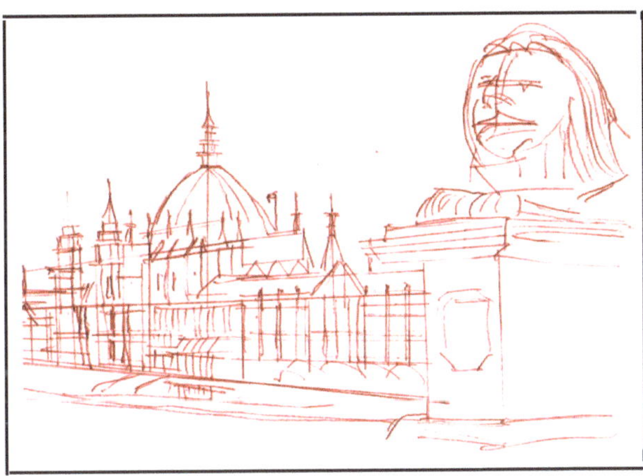

Using your markers, we can first apply color to the objects in the drawing -- mainly the building. For these objects, the colors used are Sienna, Yellow, Warm Gray 2, and Grass Green.

On the following pages I will describe applying color to complete the other parts of the drawing.

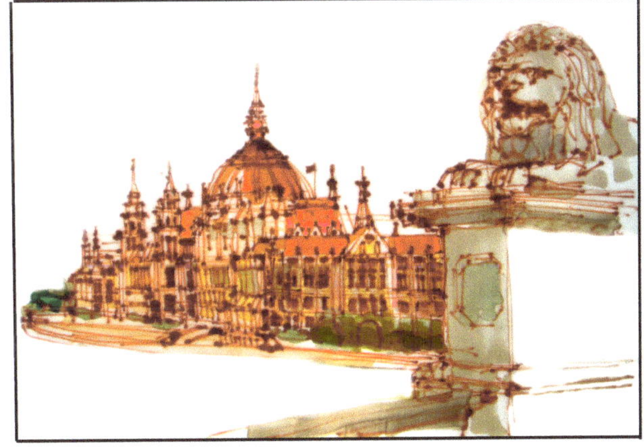

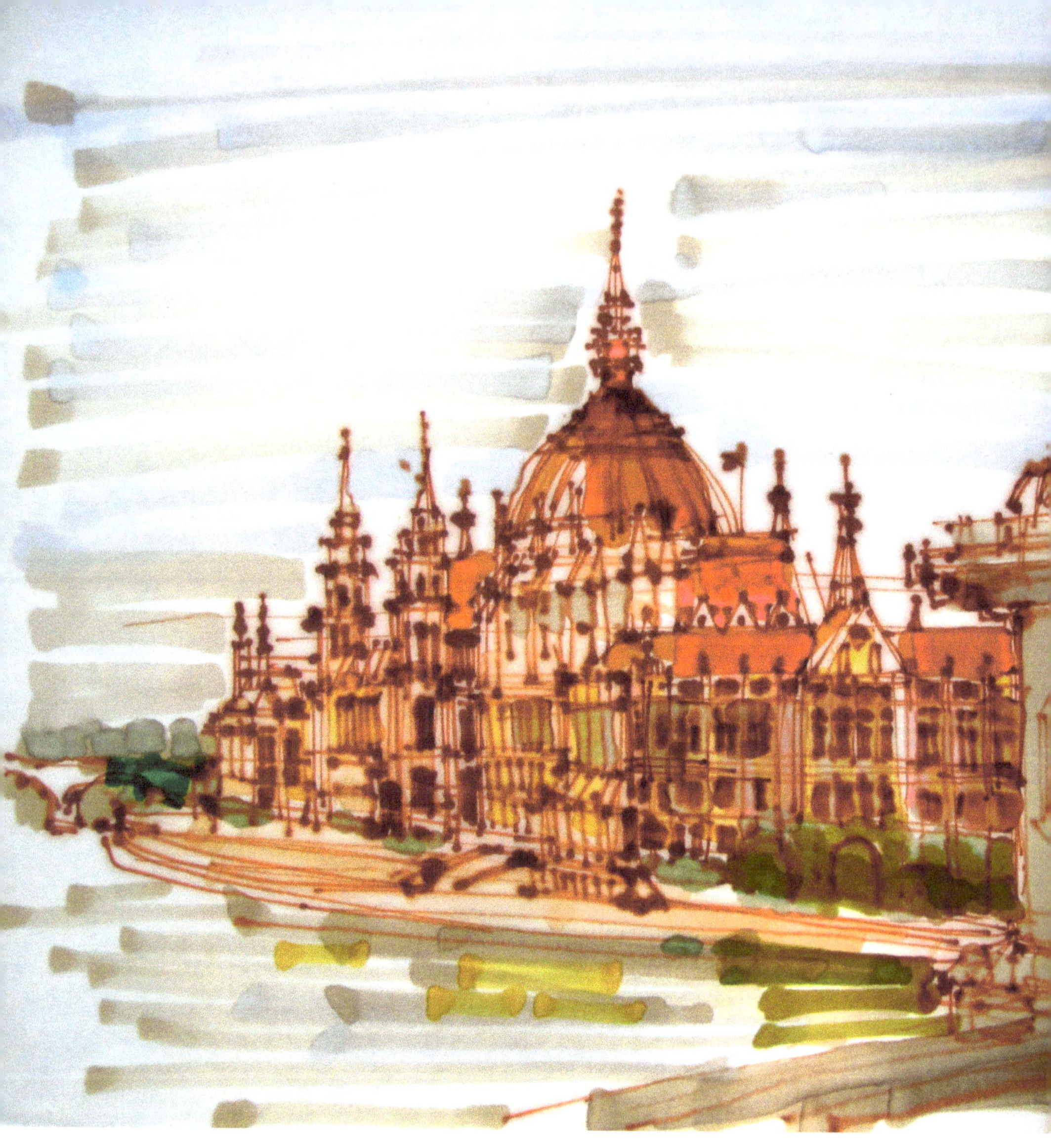

My hotel window in Budapest, Hungary afforded me a view of the Danube River with Buda on one side and Pest on the other side.

The Budapest Parliament Building was within walking distance of the hotel and I knew it would be a good subject to sketch, so I walked over to the bridge that spanned the Danube and where I could get a good view of the building with one of the bridge's pillars in the foreground.

I sketched as I saw the scene, using the pillar and stone lion as a foreground and dimensional object, and spent the early evening drawing the layout and

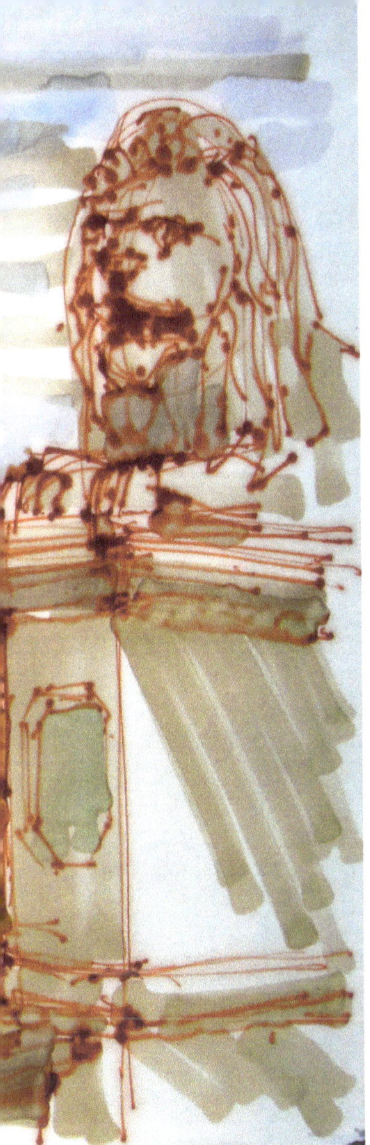

The easiest way to introduce the color of water without spending an inordinate amount of time, is to use quick strokes of Willow Green, Warm Gray 2, and colors that reflect the color of the objects near the shore. Notice the water reflections of green from the bushes and the yellowish color of the building.

Now apply color to the sky. My recommendation is the color Warm Grey 2, along with the color Saphire Blue. Although it may not be a clear, sunny day, you may wish to take artistic license and use more blue color in the sky than actually what appears to the eye.

We all have our own painting techniques, but my feeling is that the most effective technique for sketching while traveling is using a "sketchy look." This means not filling in color everywhere. It is most effective to use swift open strokes with the markers leaving white space in between the strokes. Leave white areas and use the markers and their colors only where color is useful. I often put down a base color such as pink for the front of a building, and then overlap it with a light gray in order to tone down the brightness.

It is tempting to keep adding color and "over-work" the drawing. But most drawings that still have that sketchy appearance are the most successful from your travel experience.

windows, roof and domes of this magnificent Parliament Building. As happens often, while standing on the bridge, several people gathered around to watch me draw and the children watching were especially fascinated.

From the sketch I was able to get good practice with my perspective and proportions of windows, spires, domes and other elements of the architecture. This large building is ornamented with neo Gothic turrets and arches, making it truly fascinating to draw. I felt that making this particular drawing was one of the most interesting parts of my Budapest trip and I'll always have the memories that go along with it.

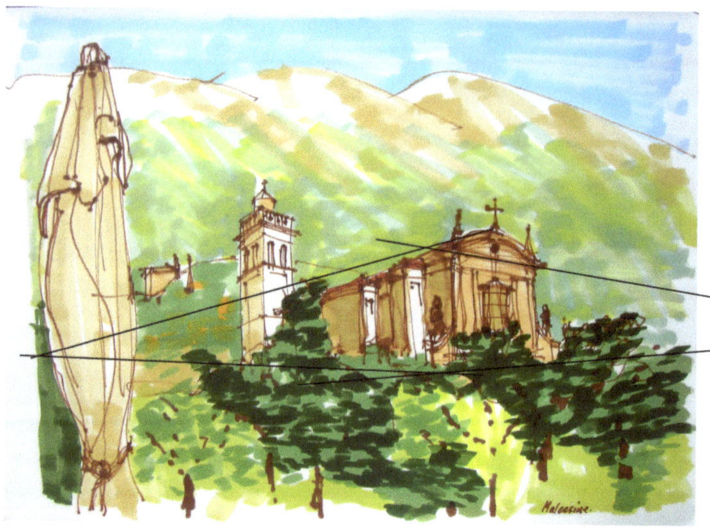

Malcesine is a town at the northeastern part of Lake Garda in Italy. From the town there is a cable-car that takes you to the top of Mount Baldo. I was there at the end of May and there was still snow on top where the ski area had recently been closed.

I hiked along a path toward the top of the mountain, which was an interesting way to see the northern part of Italy with snowcapped mountains in the background. During my hike, I found the Church of Saint Stephen Malcesine, which had an interesting architectural style.

I placed the church in the center of my sketch. My angle of perspective uses the vanishing points shown here in 2-point perspective. Notice that I use the umbrella on the left to create depth in the drawing.

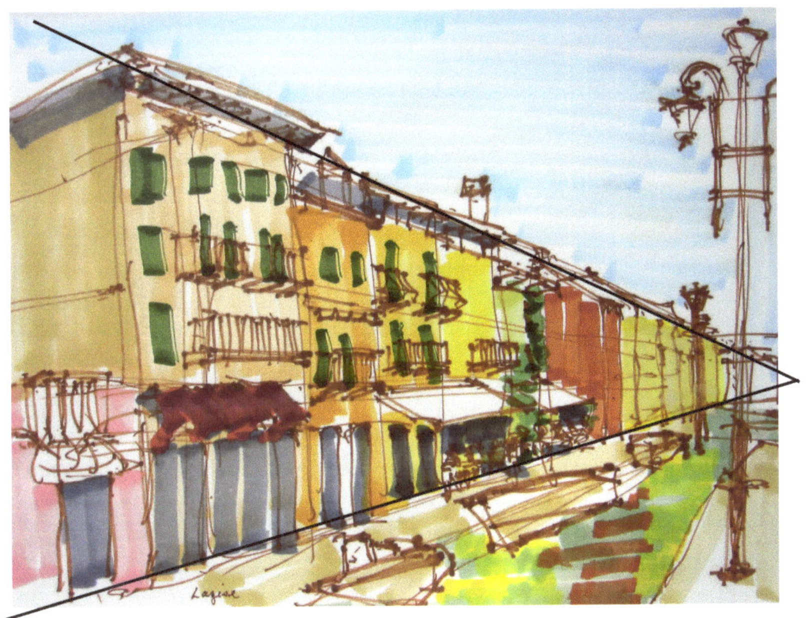

This long row of colorful facades in Lazise is sketched in 1-point perspective, emphasizing the relationship of the structures and the adjacent canal.

Lazise, a small town on Lake Garda, Italy has a series of buildings along a canal that works its way into the lake. To me, these buildings conveyed a special charm with their bright colors, balconies, and storefront activities. Also, it was interesting to watch the boats go up and down the canal, passing the structures that I was sketching. Through these drawings, I retain a visualization of the particular layout of the town and its details, such as the streetlamps and the balconies that to me were very unique.

1-POINT PERSPECTIVE

Drawing in 1-point perspective is common when the subject is viewed straight on, such as looking at the wall of a building, a room interior, or looking down something long like a canal, road or alleyway.

For a 1-point perspective, everything on the sides, top and bottom of the drawing heads towards ONE imaginary vanishing point. This is the eye level point that is located directly in front of your eyes while you are drawing.

For the layout of the subject that you have selected, make small lines on your drawing paper to show the highest point that your subject will appear, the lowest point that your subject will appear and the side points of the subject you wish to appear on your drawing.

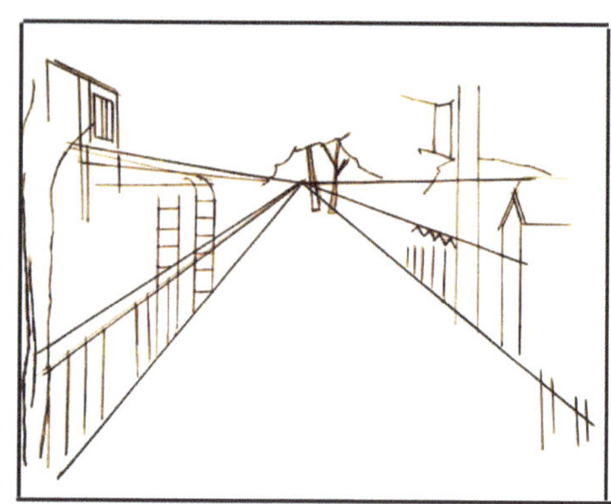

Use your straight edge or ruler and determine the horizontal angles from the scene or structure that will make up your drawing. These angles will lead you to one imaginary vanishing point. All the horizontal lines in your drawing will be based on angles that eventually reach this imaginary vanishing point.

Once you have framed in your elements on your drawing paper, all the lines that define the objects coming toward you will flow from the imaginary vanishing point.

Now determine the proportional distances on your drawing paper from one part of the subject to the next part of the subject and make vertical lines on your paper to represent those distances. On your paper, put in the line work that represents each of these items and their distance from one another. Lightly draw in these lines and the drawings will take on their three dimensional effect on your two dimensional paper.

The next step is to start adding and connecting more lines and curves to the lines that you made on your paper. The elements of your drawing are now taking shape into specific structural elements.

With your pencil or fine marker, add details such as windows, doors, tables or any items that make up the elements for your drawing. Your sketch has now been laid out in line work. If you feel the layout and the proportions of the elements work well, it is now time to add the layer of color.

Using your markers, apply color to the objects in the drawing. For this drawing, the colors used are Willow Green, Grass Green, Olive, Warm Grey 2 and 4, Umber, Pink and Saphire Blue.

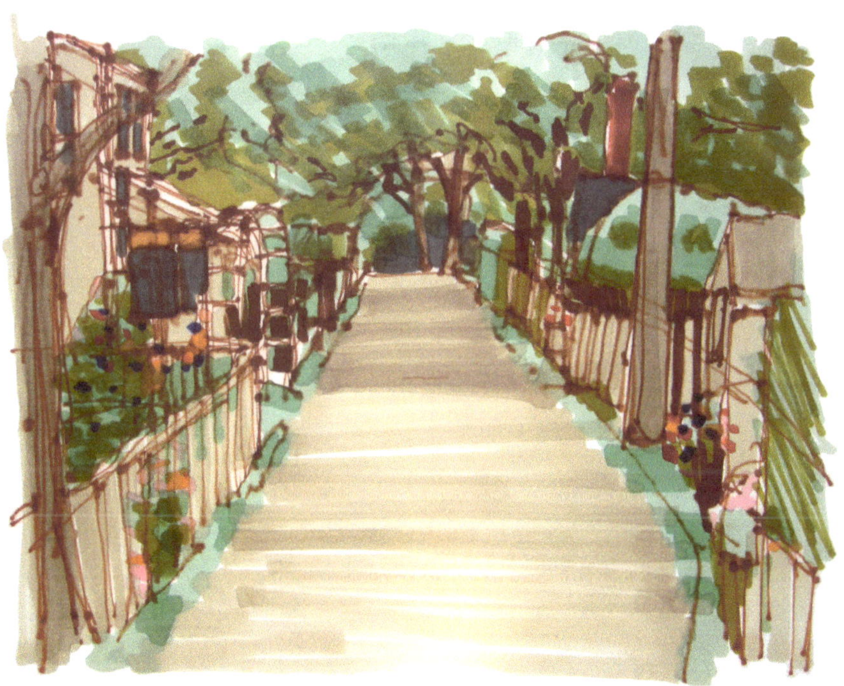

1-POINT PERSPECTIVE

The Muslim Quarter reflects the rich culture within Jerusalem. It consists of a long stretch of walking stones and steps in the old city. Some of it passes commercial areas where stores are selling every type of product imaginable, foodstuffs, grain, clothing, merchandise, religious objects and even toys. The commercial areas can be overwhelming to draw, so settling in a quieter part of the Quarter where there are a combination of residences and a few stores, including cafés, are more conducive to sketching.

With this situation, use the same sketching technique as shown on the previous page. From the view of the subject that you have selected, make small lines on your drawing paper to show the highest point that your subject will appear, the lowest point that your subject will appear and the side points of the subject you wish to appear on your drawing.

Use your straight edge or ruler and determine the horizontal angles from the scene that will make up your drawing. These angles will lead you to one imaginary vanishing point.

Now determine the proportional distances on your drawing paper from one part of the subject to the next part of the subject and make lines on your paper to represent those distances. On your paper, put in the line work that represents each of these items and their distance from one another.

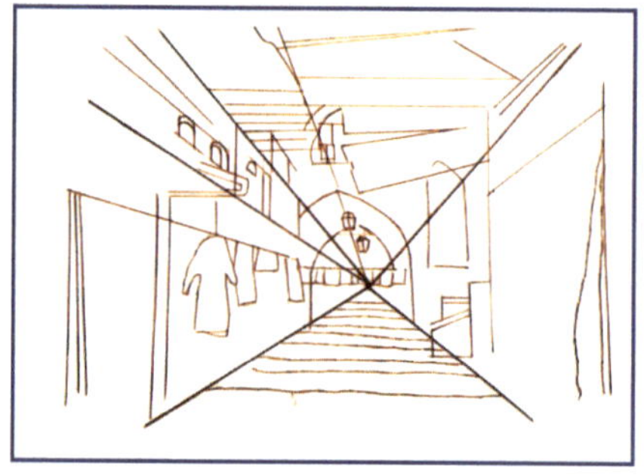

With your pencil or fine marker, add details such as arches, windows, or any items that make up the elements for your drawing. If you feel the layout and the proportions of the elements work well, it is now time to add the layer of color.

Using your markers, apply color to the objects in the drawing. For this drawing, the colors used are Pale Sepia, Saphire Blue, Redwood, Scarlet, Pink, and Warm Grays 2, 4 and 7.

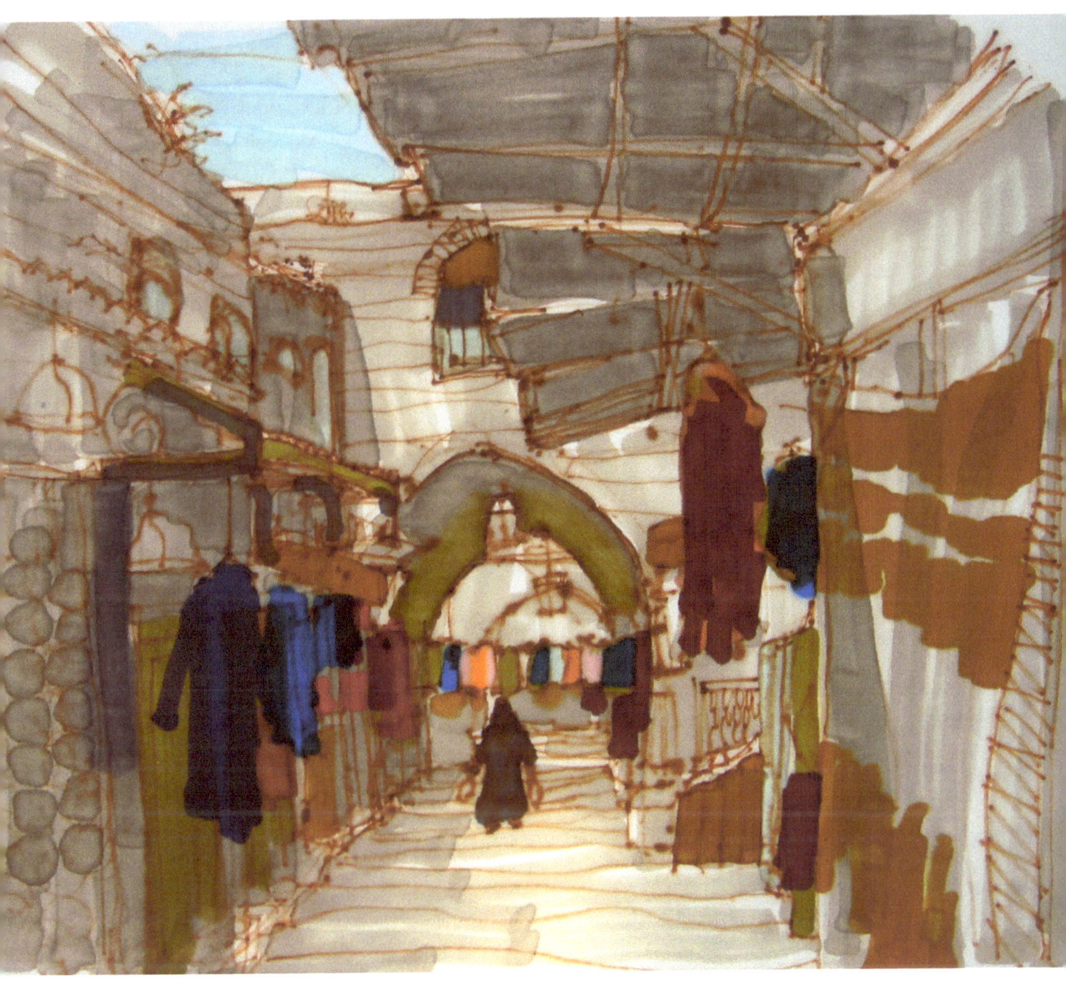

1-POINT PERSPECTIVE

Since Aix-en-Provence in France has so many markets, it seemed like there was always an interesting place to draw. I was determined to sketch either a flower market or a food market, so I started walking around the main part of town. Arriving at the main square, I found it packed with people. There were tour groups with their leaders holding signs, some in English, some Chinese, some German and some French. I couldn't imagine how I was going to sketch around these crowded markets or even find a place to set up a sketch pad, so I kept walking and found a small raised area by the flower market where a series of motorcycles were parked, and which presented a clearing for me and my sketch pad.

I had found the scene that I wanted to sketch, and rested my sketch pad on one of the parked motorcycle seats and started sketching. I established the highest part of the sketch -- just above the umbrella -- and the lowest part just below the planters in the foreground. After then establishing the side points for the subject to draw, I was ready to address the use of perspective as shown on the opposite page.

After framing out the layout and sketching with the pointed marker, applying the flower colors with rhe flat-nib markers immediately brightened up the picture. The flower market was busy and hectic with the changing light and the changing flowers and the changing people. As soon as I started drawing some bunches of flowers, the flowers were sold and they then disappeared. Fortunately, the umbrellas stayed in place!

Surrounded by motorcyles while I was drawing, several people – tourists and kids – passed this motorcycle parking area and seemed to enjoy watching me and commenting.

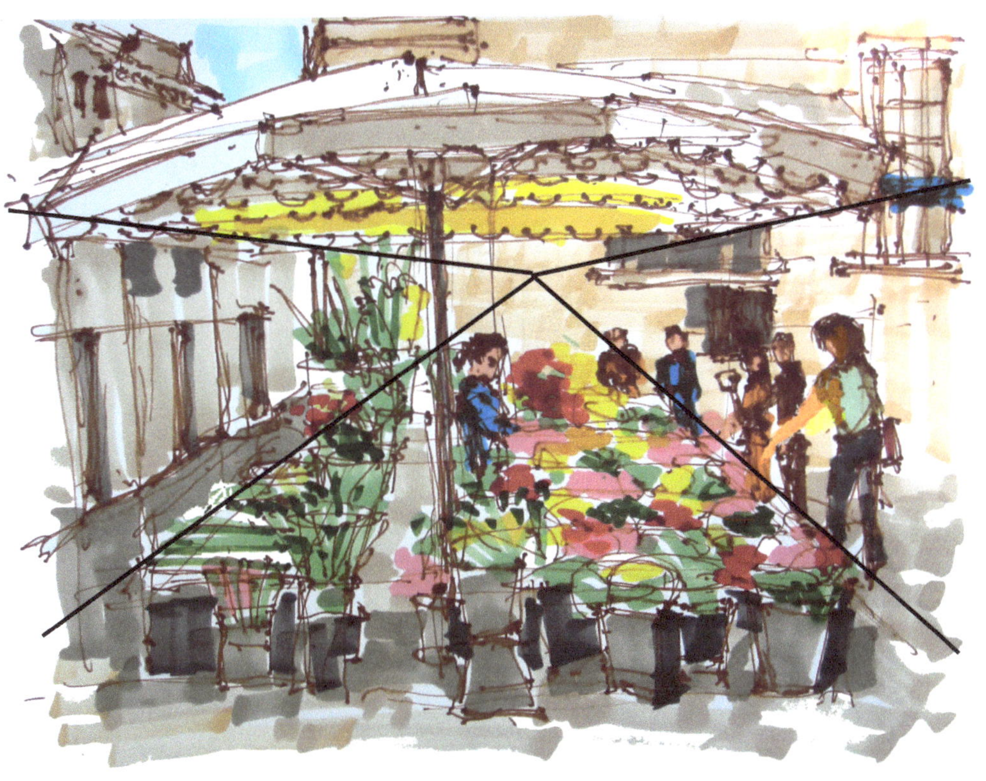

The four black lines that overprint this sketch indicate the use of 1-point perspective and the single vanishing point in the center. Those lines follow the main elements of the drawing -- the large umbrellas and the flower-selling area. This establishes the view that the artist will use for the sketch.

Bonnieux, France

Bonnieux was my favorite town in Provence. The town is perched on a narrow steep ridge rising up from a flat plane toward the 12th century church at the top of the plane with its high, pointed steeple. The village is full of picturesque old streets, fountains, shops and medieval walls as well as cafés and restaurants. In this hillside village there is much walking up and down.

With many gorgeous buildings, winding streets, alleyways, archways and pastures below and with mountains in the background, I was truly inspired to sketch and wanted to capture the feeling of being there, not only from its mountain perspective but also from the perspective of its steps and alleyways.

This drawing was from the top of a long series of steps. I found a place to rest my drawing pad and markers on top of a low stone wall and proceeded to sketch looking down the pathway, toward the houses and the mountains in the background. Although the shadows moved during the time I was drawing, I was able to use the shadows to give dimension to the drawing. With my markers, I concentrated on the color of the buildings, the shadows, the roof tiles and the field below.

When drawing this type of scene, it's preferable to set your perspective from a single focal point. For this drawing, my focal point was the center of the drawing at the bottom of the pathway.

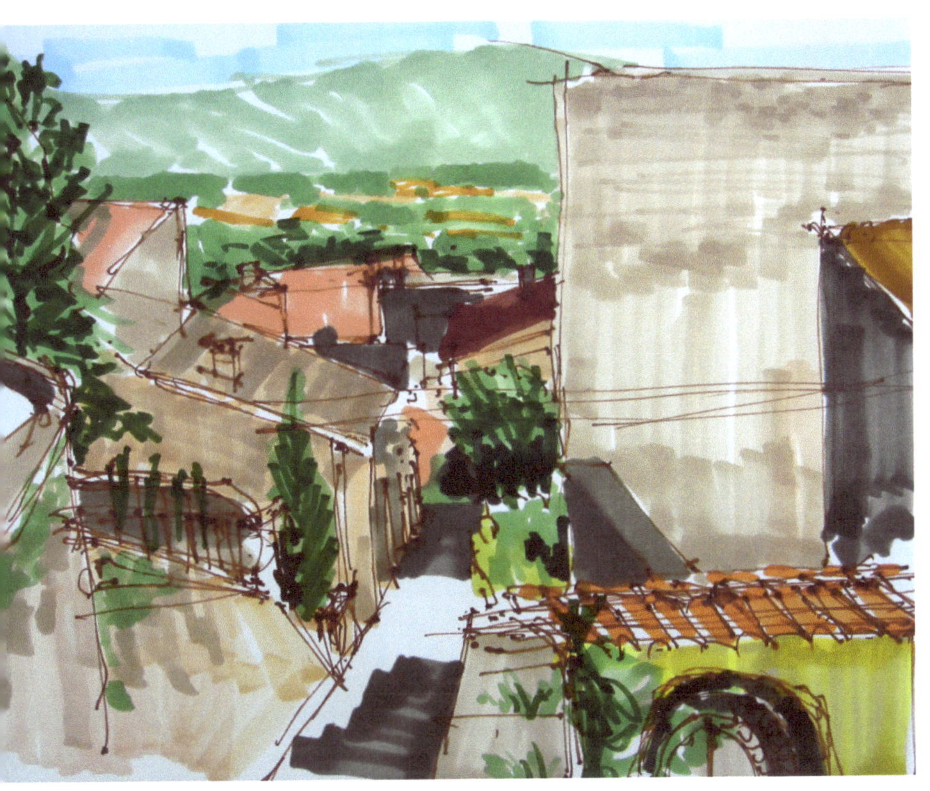

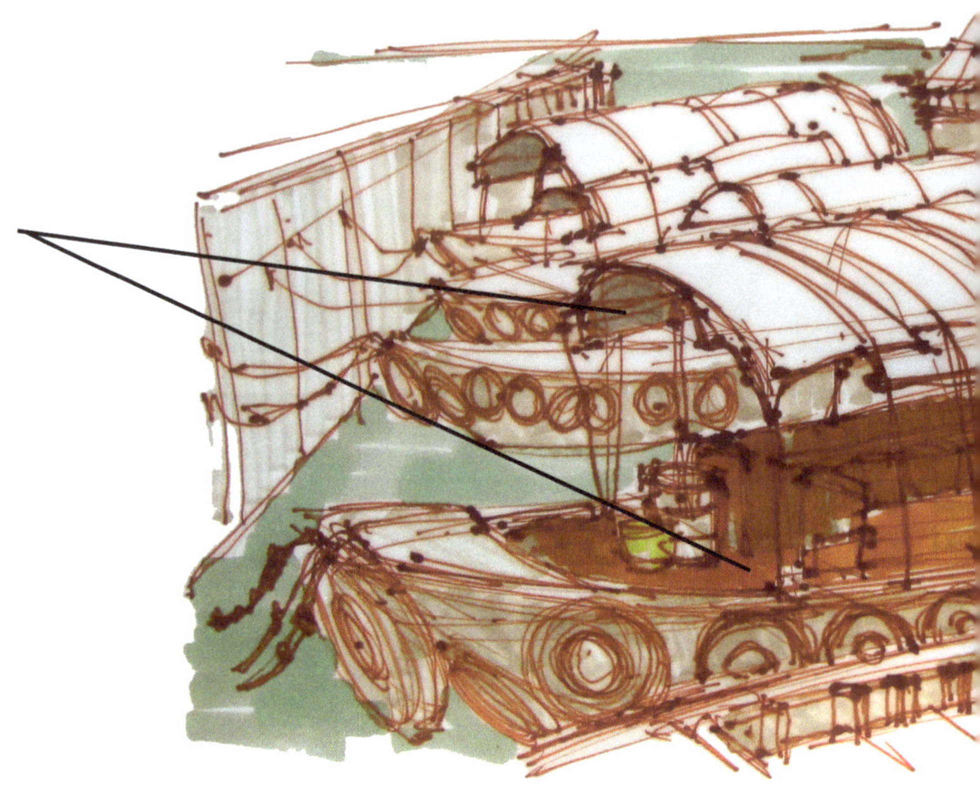

Aberdeen Harbor, Hong Kong

Hong Kong and its islands are an artist's paradise. Here at Aberdeen Harbor there was a line of sampans that were used for sightseeing and general transportation from island to island. From my view on the dock, I used 2-point perspective with imaginary vanishing points.

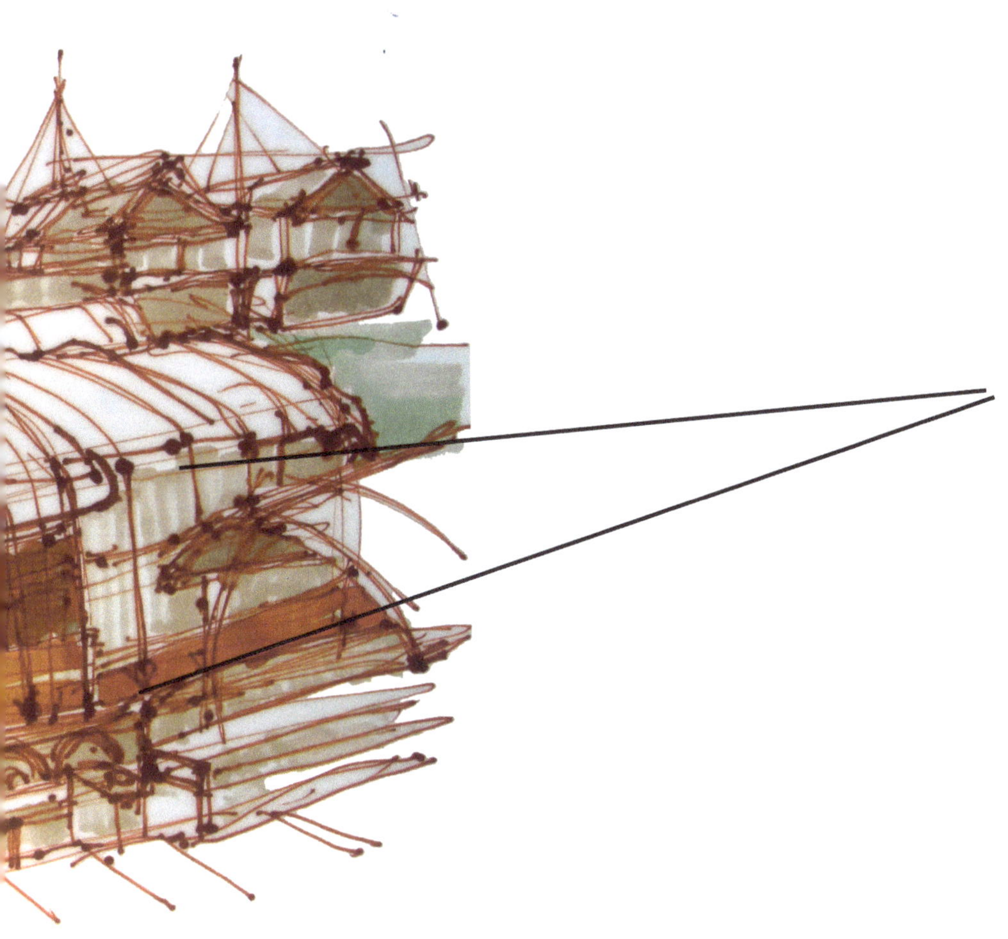

With their shapes and large canopies the boats formed an interesting scene, and by sketching them I could understand how these boats were built. They added to the uniqueness of Hong Kong, and I wanted to capture their spirit with the drawing.

Shadows and Shading

An interesting part of your sketching while traveling is capturing the shadows that will appear in your drawings. Since many of your drawings will be outdoors, the light will change during the day and the shadows change as the sun moves. Even if your drawing takes you less than one hour, the shadows will have moved from where you had started the drawing. Don't worry about it. The main thing to remember is that the shading and the shadows help define the shapes of the items that you are drawing. Especially on a sunny day, it is advantageous to really take advantage of those shaded and shadow areas so that the color you use on the non-shaded area will contrast to the color you use on the shaded area. Any subject, whether a building, statue, wall, or even a mountain can be strongly defined by the shadows and the shading that you will use.

In most cases your shading areas can be accomplished by using the Gray marker as an overlay to the color of the item. For example, when I draw a house, the lighted side of the house might be a light gray and the shaded part a darker gray. The addition of a shadow on the ground or a shadow from the trees will lend dimension to your drawing and make it more interesting.

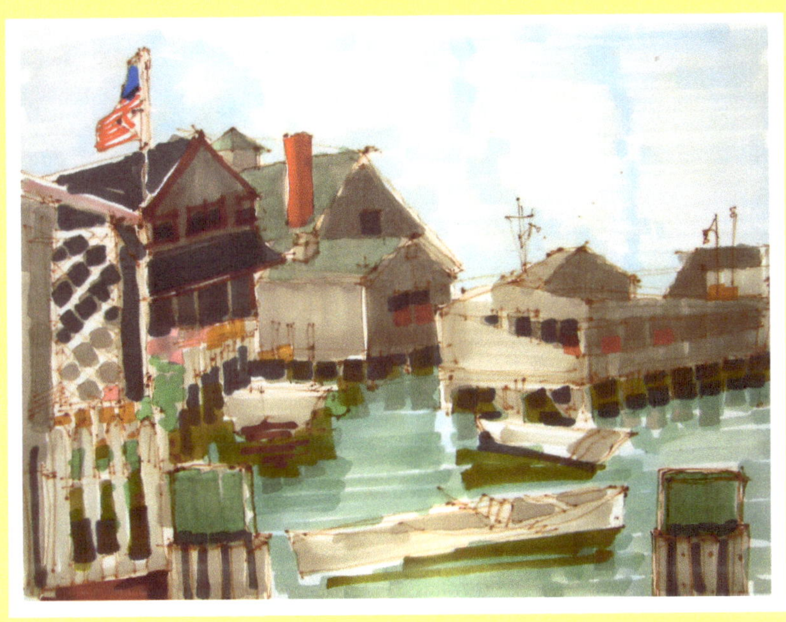

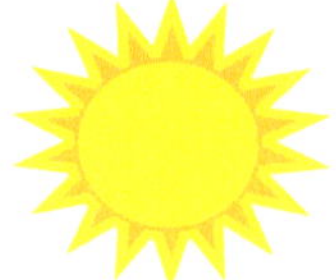

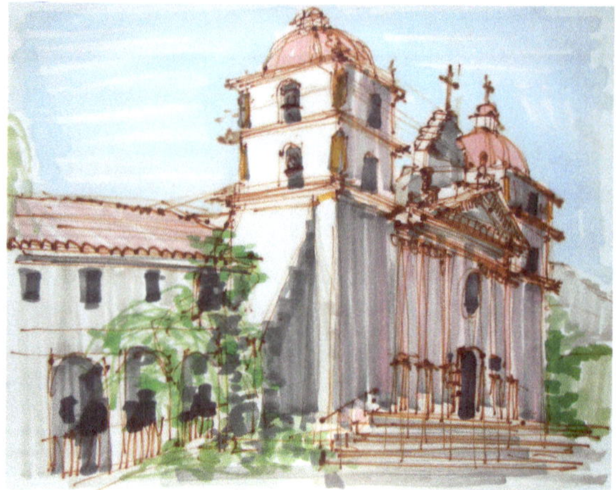

Keep in mind that if your light source, or the sun, is coming from a particular angle, the brightness should appear on every part of every object that's facing that angle. The shadows and shading should appear on the opposite side from that light source and be consistently applied. Specifically, if the light source is coming from the left side of the house, the shadow will be on the right side of the house as you see in these drawings.

In each of my drawings, I have handled the shadows in a slightly different manner --- you will note that they are all done without complete accuracy – the shading and the shadows still have a sketchy effect but enable you to see the strong dimension of the subjects in the sketch.

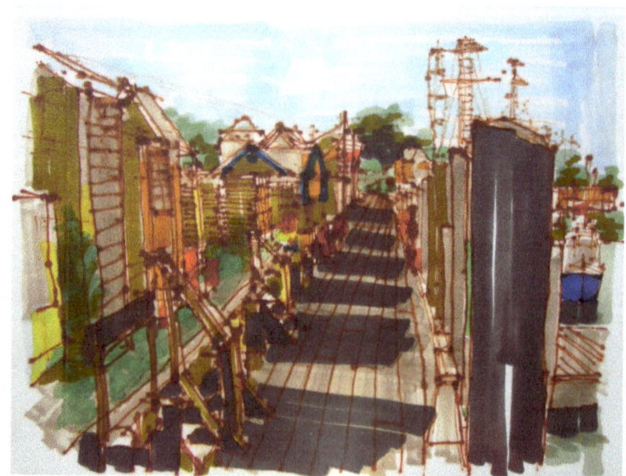

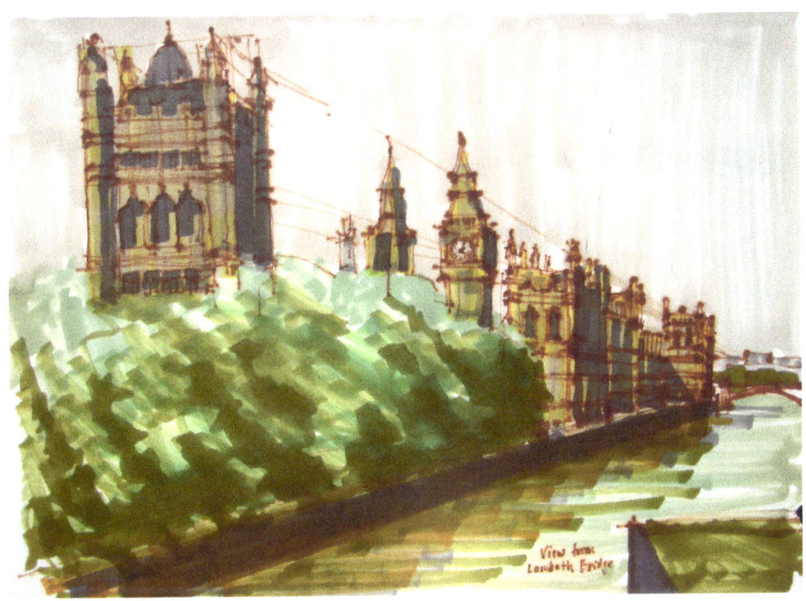

A bridge view that is rarely missed by visitors to London is the view along the Thames River from Lambeth Bridge, which looks over the Houses of Parliament along with the famous Big Ben. I became familiar with some of these buildings from seeing many photographs of London through the years.

As I've mentioned, making a drawing is quite different from taking a photograph, since you really get to study the towers in the structures and the placement of the clock, the placement of the windows and the afternoon shadows. I could not resist taking the time to make this drawing while standing on this bridge and leaning my sketchpad against a side rail on the walkway.

Muslim Quarter, Jerusalem

The Muslim Quarter, Jerusalem, has a long path of walking stones and steps in the old city. It passes through commercial areas with carts and stores along with some residential sections. After touring the area, I settled on the quieter parts of the Quarter where the combination of residences and a few stores served as cafés and fabric markets.

My son Bruce and I stopped and took chairs within two different sections of this walkway which gave me the opportunity to draw and observe the fascinating elements of two sections of the Muslim Quarter – both sections with stone steps, wood framing, stone buildings in the background, arches, lanterns, and the clothing that would hang from the various structures within the walkway.

The steps lead down to parts of the Quarter that went from outdoors to indoors. The light that was cast allowed for some interesting colors – still muted, but interesting. You will note the gold color of Jerusalem stone on the left part of the top drawing and then moving into more muted and gray colors due to the shadows that were cast by the arches and the various structures. To introduce scale, I wanted to show people walking down the stairs as well as climbing up the stairs. Although several details are shown in these drawings, I kept the simplest forms in the arches, steps, walls, and ceiling.

The colors in the lower drawing are somewhat muted as was the scene itself, mostly ochers, tans and grays, with the clothing adding color to the drawing. To me that was the interesting element – the fact that most of the color was added by the clothing that hung in the scene.

Beams of light came from the roof into the narrow quarter, since it was not fully enclosed -- which cast the shadows and shading for a dramatic effect.

This was a fascinating part of the world to capture as a drawing and to have the opportunity to really see those details such as the arches, steps, lanterns, railings, wood framework and all the elements that I was able to study while making these drawings.

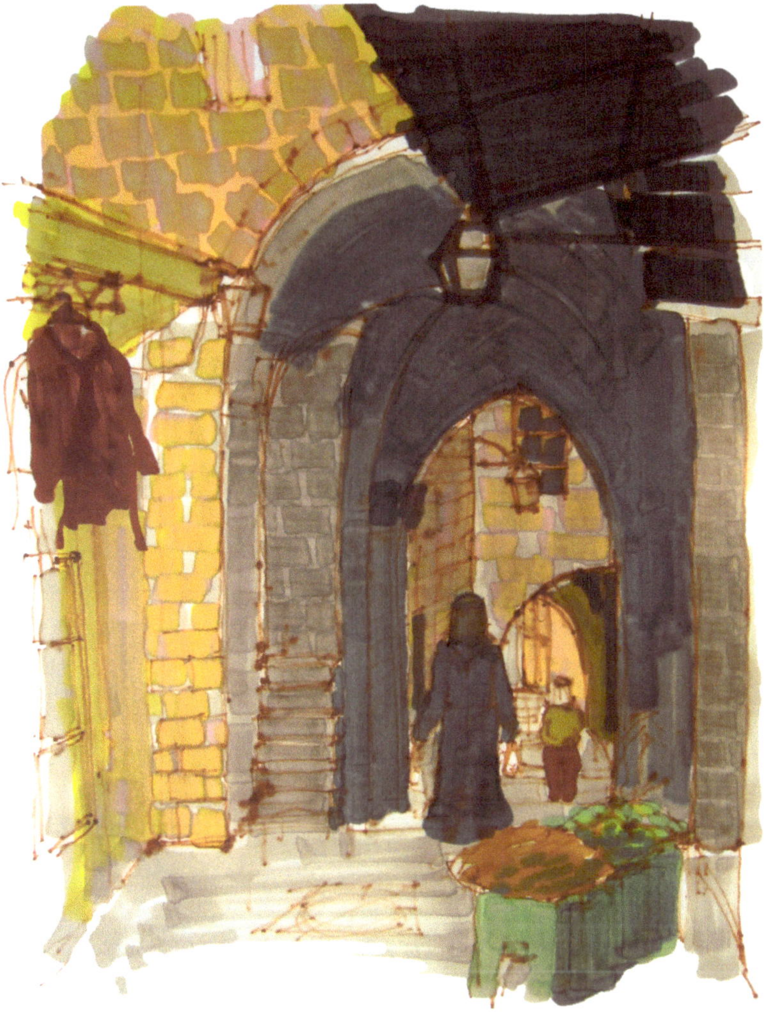

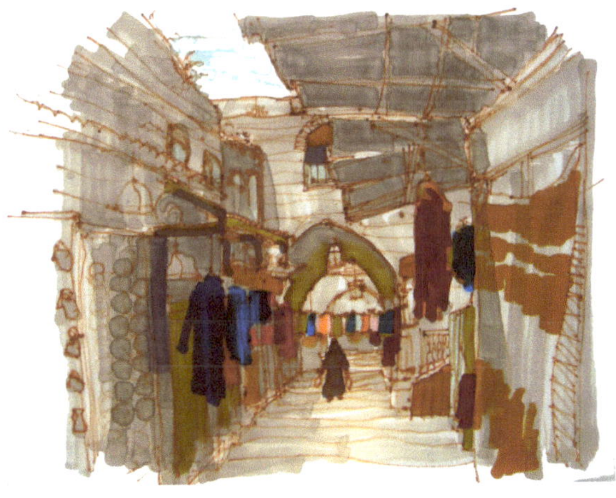

Sketching with the iPad

The iPad is the ultimate drawing surface for portability and color.   There are many apps for drawing on the iPad – my favorite apps for ease of use are "Brushes Redux", "Procreate", and "Sketchbook." Before you start sketching in the style shown on this page, get familiar with the drawing interface on your iPad. Turn the following page and you will find a brief description of the interface for "Brushes Redux." With variations, other drawing apps have similar interfaces.

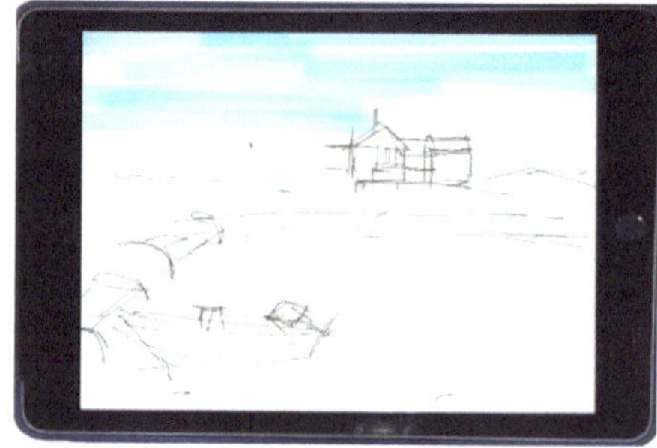

After determining the scene and layout for your sketch, put in your line work and then add the color. The drawing apps give you an unlimited variety of brush widths, colors and textures to use for your sketching – they also enable you to erase as often as you wish.

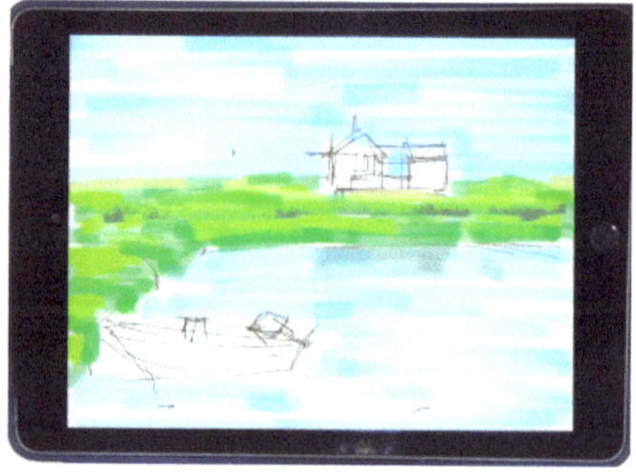

Be sure to practice sketching with it before you take it on the road. The iPad proved to be for me a convenient and portable way to move around places like India for sketching. However, there are pros and cons to keep in mind when drawing on an iPad or on any electronic tablet:

The main pro is its portability. Instead of carrying a large drawing pad with a set of several dozen markers, paints or brushes, the iPad is self-contained and lightweight. The colors are unlimited. You can use a stylus (about $10) to draw in your lines and colors. You can email your drawings to friends and relatives as you complete the drawing. You can print the drawings in any size.

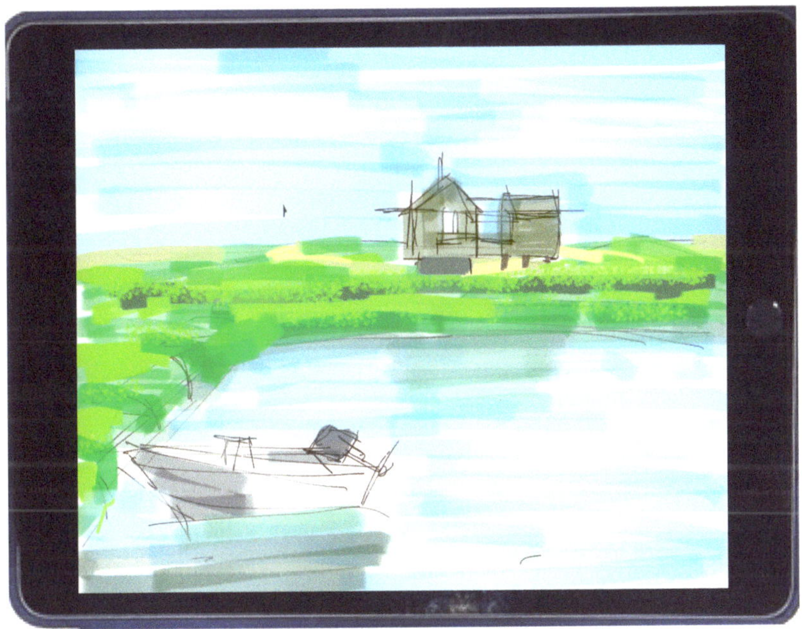

A disadvantage of the electronic tablet is the difficulty of gauging accurate colors in direct sunlight because of reflection on the glass surface. I some-times look for a shady spot from which to sketch. At times I've resorted to wearing a wide-brimmed sun-hat to cast a shadow on the iPad when I work.

When I get home I usually make an 8x10 print from my iPad drawing and then print it larger at a copy center for framing. I set a limit to the prints made and sign and number the prints on the front. I recently saw a museum exhibit of iPad drawing prints by the international artist David Hockney, who enlarged his iPad prints to 3 feet by 4 feet!

iPAD DRAWING INTERFACE

The drawing app interface shown on the opposite page is from the "Brushes Redux" app on the iPad. With variations, other drawing apps, such as "Procreate" and "Sketchbook" have similar interfaces. You may wish to experiment with the different drawing apps to determine your preference.

Before sketching on an iPad, you will need to familiarize yourself with the attributes of the elements that give you brush shapes, brush sizes, colors, erasing, and other drawing features. It's really not difficult, but it does take some practice before you confidently enjoy sketching with the iPad.

With your stylus, start by tapping on the BRUSH ICON for a selection of brush shapes.

Then tap on your preferred brush shape and slide the SIZE GAUGE to the brush size you prefer: 2 px (pixels) give you a pencil-thin line, 15 px a medium size, and 30 px or more for large brush widths.

Color Selection

Tap the COLOR RECTANGLE on the left for colors to appear. You will see a combination of color wheel, color palette, and small palette boxes. From the color wheel, you can mix the color you want and drag it into one of the small palette boxes for use on your drawing.

You can change the darkness and the transparency of each color by using the TRANSPARENCY SLIDER under the color wheel. There is also an eraser tool that you can use.

The best way to start sketching with the iPad is by practicing simple drawings, such as a vase or a chair. Once you get the hang of sketching on the iPad, you will find that it is not only challenging but also it is fun!

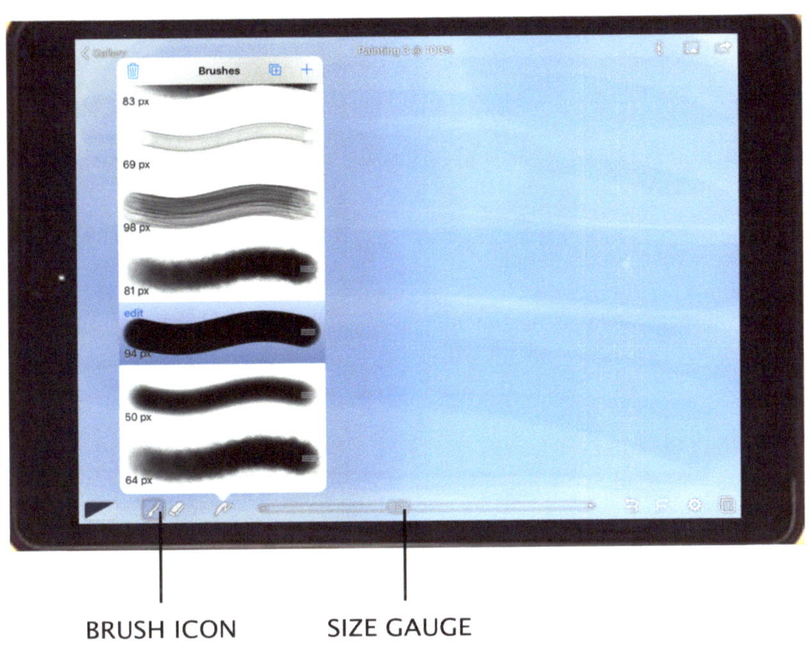

BRUSH ICON   SIZE GAUGE

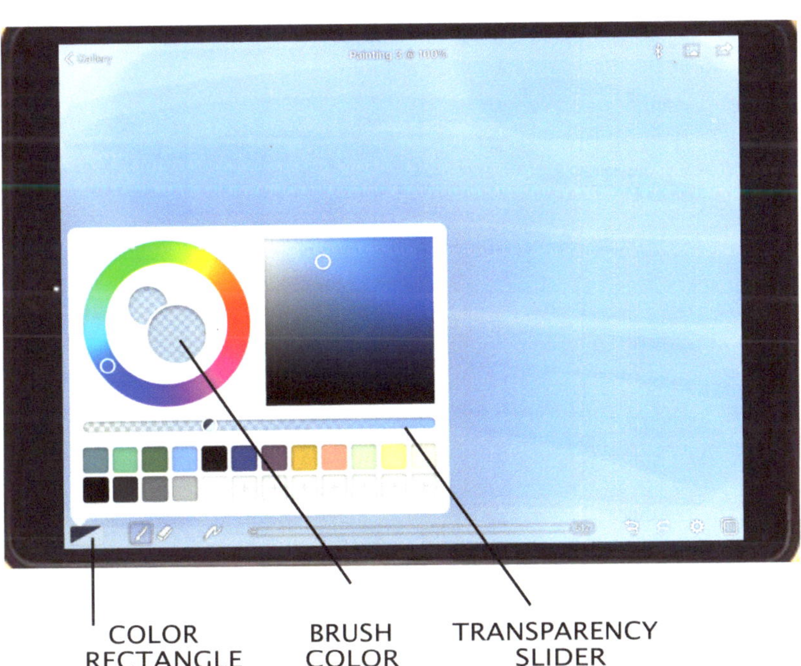

COLOR RECTANGLE   BRUSH COLOR   TRANSPARENCY SLIDER

iPAD PAINTBRUSH METHOD

Another way to sketch using the iPad is with a "paintbrush" method. Since the iPad provides an electronic pallet of different size paintbrushes, here is the way it can be done.

Select one of the electronic paintbrushes along with the color that will be used on your sky. Then fill in the sky.

Now mark your horizontal and vertical points, along with your horizon line and form the outline of your subject in the color that it will eventually become.

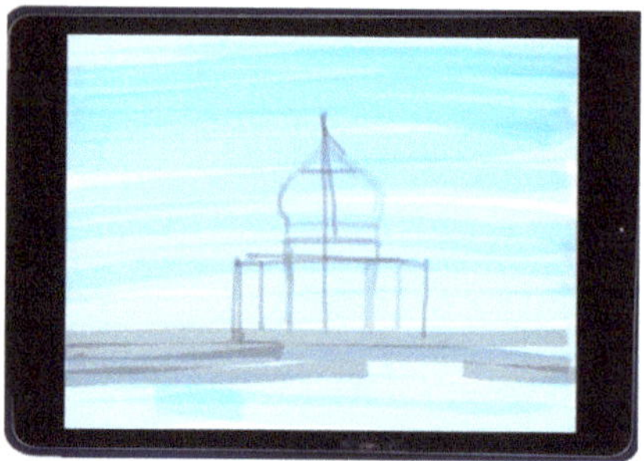

Then fill in the subject with the colors as you would do in a painting, using colors from your electronic pallet. Your base colors are now on your iPad and you can erase or add colors as you see fit.

Finally, add in the details as shown on the opposite page, using colors from your electronic pallet. As I've said, all this takes practice but the result (see next page) is worth it!

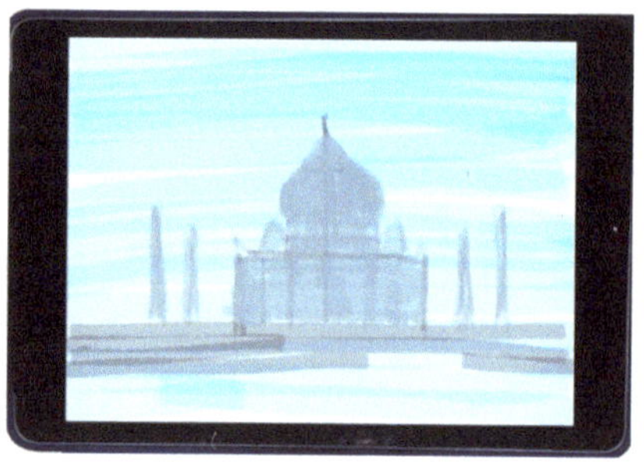

OUR TRIP TO INDIA was going to not only be a trip of a lifetime but also the trip in which to do a lot of drawing. When drawing in India and many parts of Asia, you find that people are not accustomed to seeing artists sketching, and they often gather politely near you to watch. Additionally, if you want someone to pose in your drawing or wish to show someone's home or store in your drawing, they may expect to receive a small tip as a thank-you for their participation.

We were fortunate to have had a private tour for the 2 1/2 weeks that we were there, consisting of various drivers in various regions. Most of my drawings were done during time off when we were on our own and we would go over to the scenes and spend an hour or so making the sketch.

The Taj Mahal drawing was an exception. Throughout the trip I was looking

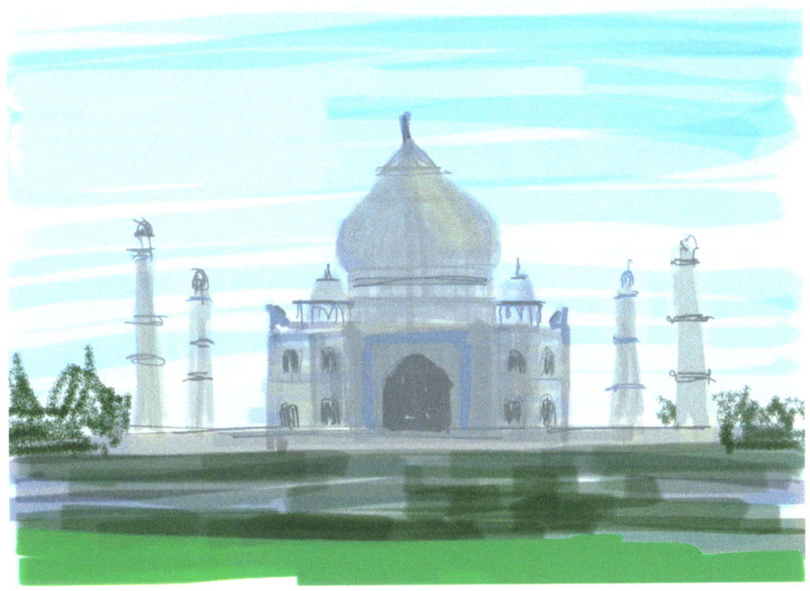

forward to making this drawing, and when it came time to take a tour of the Taj Mahal, I was told that I was not allowed to use this electronic tablet – iPad – in the grounds of this extraordinary structure. I was quite disappointed but the guide told me that he would take us early the next morning across the pond from the Taj Mahal to a park that overlooks the Taj Mahal, from which I could sit comfortably and sketch the scene. We woke up early that next morning and went to the park and it worked out perfectly. The sun was on the other side of the Taj Mahal and the marble reflected shading that one rarely has seen. Instead of the building being white as shown on most photos, the building turned to a luxurious warm gray color with a slight mixture of yellow from the reflecting sunlight. It was not a way that I had ever seen the Taj Mahal coloration, and I went out of my way to make sure that the colors that I used on the drawing accurately reflected what I actually saw. I will always remember the marble color of the structure at the time that morning in Agra, India and my drawing reinforces the memory.

iPad Portability at Parc Guell, Barcelona

Here is a sample of the third drawing that I ever made on the iPad, which was made in Barcelona, Spain, a week after Apple sold the first iPad to the public.

In Barcelona, I was looking around for various places to draw. Unfortunately, of the five days that we spent in Barcelona, four of them were rainy, which made it impossible to make outdoor drawings with the iPad. I practiced iPad sketching in a tapas bar, and when we finally had a sunny day, we took a trip to the Parc Guell, where I found a spot to stand and make this sketch at the entrance to the park.

The park entrance was crowded with people moving and I had no place to rest the iPad. So I stood and held the iPad in my hand while sketching the scene. I could not have accomplished this with a paper sketchpad and markers.

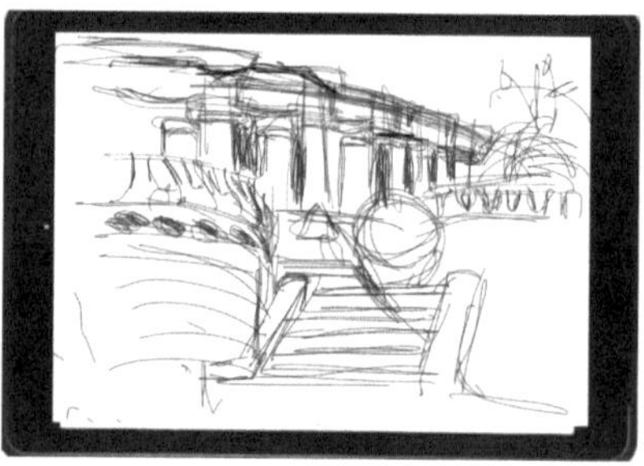

After setting up the perspective points, I first sketched in the line work that you see here. Once satisfied with the layout, I applied the color, resulting in the drawing on the following page.

I sketched quickly, which gave me the time to then enjoy walking around the park. I was happy to find that I did not have to lean the iPad on anything while sketching, and I enjoyed the new activity of iPad drawing and taking advantage of its portability.

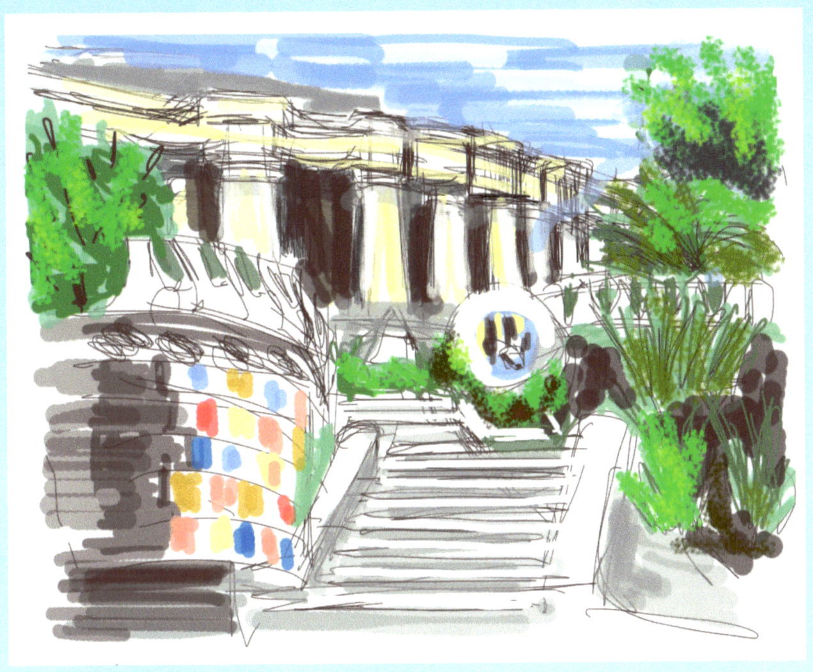

For sketching trees on the iPad, I found a technique that works most efficiently. After using thin dark lines to sketch out the scene, put one layer of Medium Green over all the trees, bushes and grass. Then, put in Dark Green for the shading. A Dark Grey or Olive color also works for shading. Then, add your lighter colors, such as Yellow Green and Yellow Ochre. This iPad technique for trees differs from the technique for sketchpad and markers where you would intrduce the lighter colors before applying the darker color shading. House colors and sky colors then complete the drawing as shown on the opposite page.

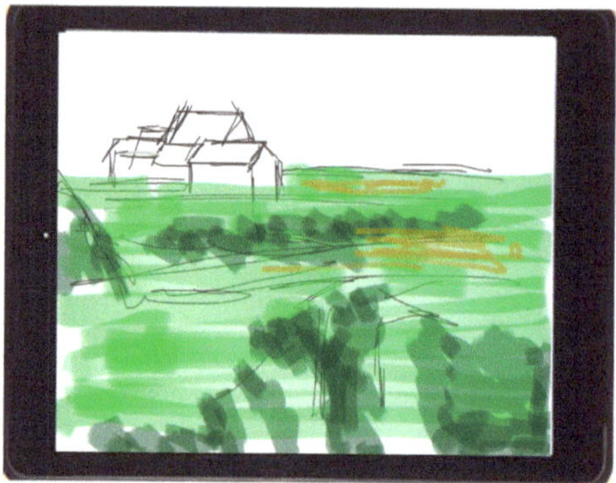

This iPad sketch was made on the western end of Nantucket Island. One thing I was able to do with the iPad -- which was not possible with my large paper sketchpad -- was standing and holding the iPad in my hand while sketching the scene. With a large paper sketchpad and many different color markers, it would have been impossible to stand on the grass and draw. When I sketch with the paper sketchpad I have to find a place in which to lean it and a place for the color markers. I was happy to find that I did not have to lean the iPad on anything, and I enjoyed the activity of iPad drawing and taking advantage of its portability.

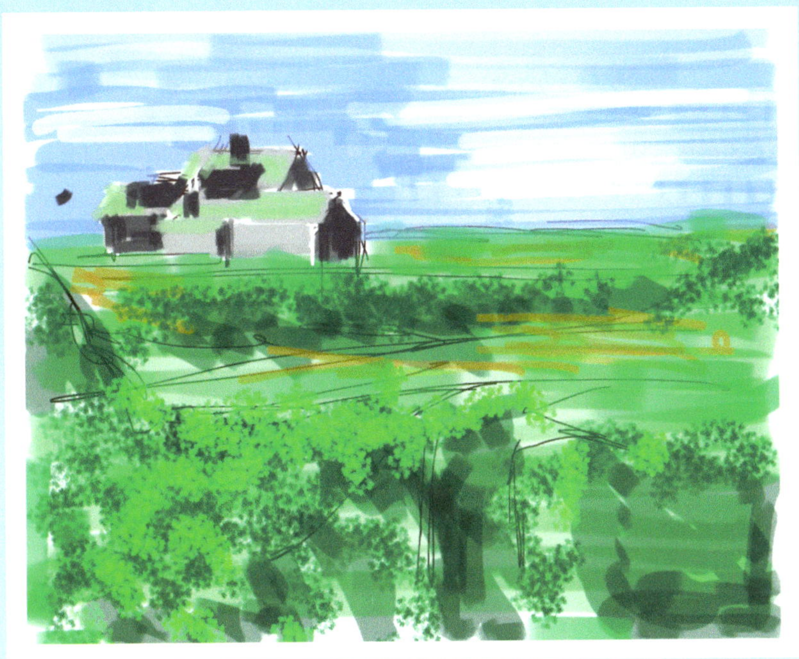

While Jo Ann was shopping nearby, I made the iPad sketch -- that you see on the opposite page -- of the Keizersgract Canal in only 20 minutes, capturing the essence of a typical Amsterdam canal. Typical architecture on the Amsterdam canals include buildings with very slim proportions. The buildings usually rest against one another and the combination of the bright structures, prominent roofs and colorful reflections in the water made for some interesting drawing.

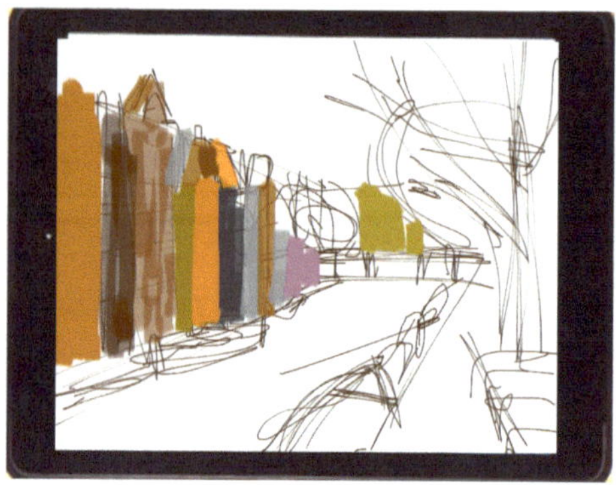

You can sketch quickly on the iPad by first using a thin line to frame out all the basic elements. This gives you the perspective and structure for the drawing. Then introduce the color to fill the open areas of the drawing. Then add the detailed elements like the trees --- first the outlines, next the Dark Green, and then the Lighter Greens to emphasize the leaves. Put reflections in the water using the colors of the buildings.

Note the transition from the sketch above to the finished iPad sketch on the opposite page. In this case, quick sketching kept me from overworking the drawing, making it spontaneous and memorable.

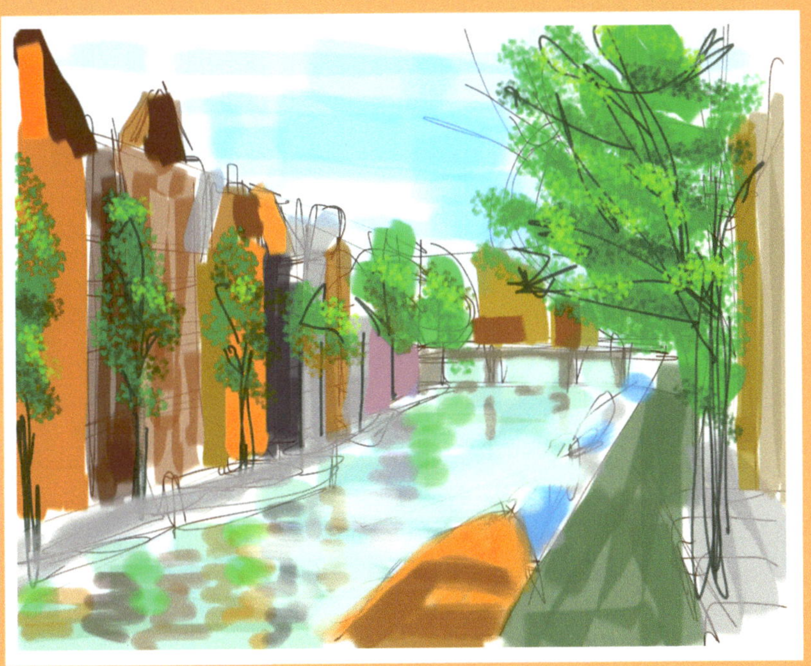

Sketching with an electronic medium, such as the iPad, gives you the opportunity to make shortcuts in your drawings.

For example, the drawing applications on the iPad enable you to make instant copies of your drawings during your sketching process. If you want to keep something that you have sketched and then make a quick variation of it, you can.

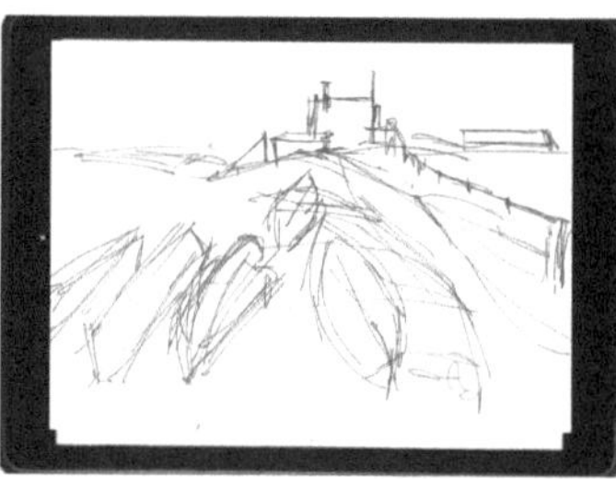

This shows my drawing of a beach at Smith's Point in Nantucket with some kayaks in the dunes. The original drawing is laid out with thin dark lines to frame the intended scene. As you see on the upper opposite page, the boats, grass, sand, fence, and house are then rendered in color. Once the drawing was completed, I wanted to show how that beachfront looked without the kayaks, since the kayaks are not always on the beach.

After electronically copying the first image, I used my stylus to erase the kayaks and add grass and sand without changing the rest of the drawing. The lower drawing was completed in less than 10 minutes.

This technique of making changes and keeping the original sketch can be applied to any sketch when using a drawing app on the iPad. My preferred apps for sketching are *Brushes Redux, SketchBook,* and *Procreate*, all of which can be found on the iPad at the Apple App Store.

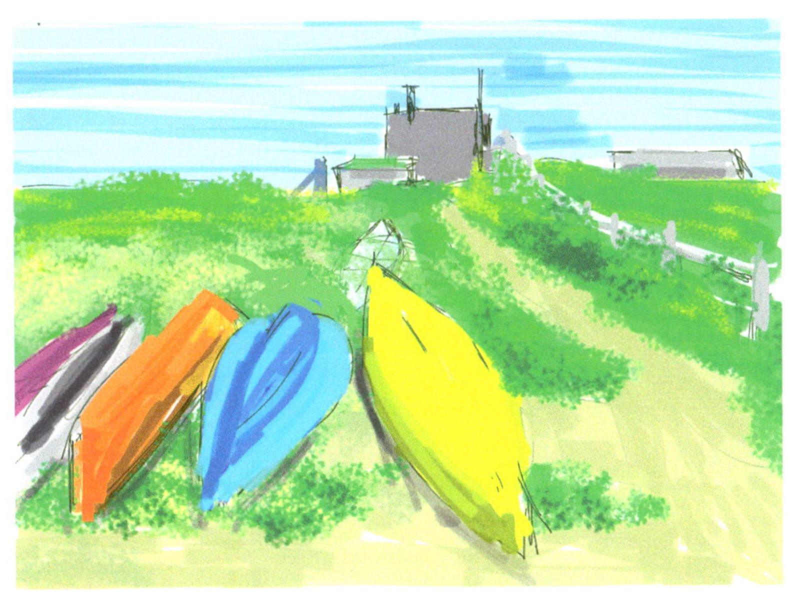

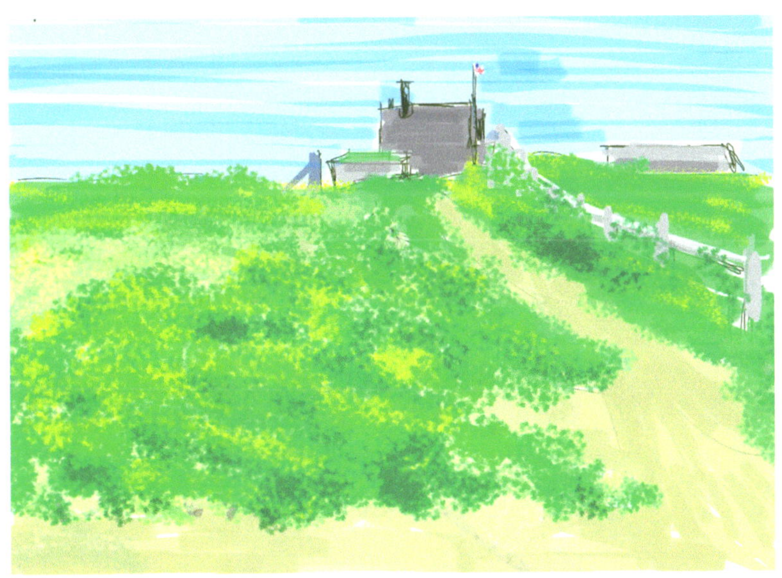

iPad Water Reflections in San Juan, PR

On a trip to San Juan, Puerto Rico I stayed at The Caribe Hilton which was located near San Juan town and on the Caribbean Sea beachfront. Walking around the hotel with my iPad, I noticed a small pond surrounded by tropical trees, which reflected many colors in the water. Impressed by the beauty of the pond, I took the opportunity to sketch this scene and experimented on the iPad with the colors that were reflected in the water.

On my iPad, I started out by framing the scene in thin dark line and then added color. You can the first blue layer below.

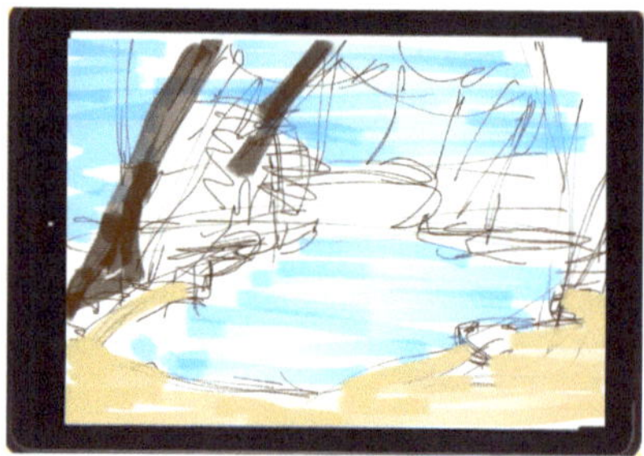

Then I started using wide color strokes to pick up the colors from the surrounding trees and bushes that you see on the following page. The pond now comes alive with these colors. Included in the pond pallet: Light Blue, Medium Blue, Leaf Green, Yellow Green, Olive and White.

The effect is sketchy and conveys the ripples and reflections that make the pond-water dimensional and interesting.

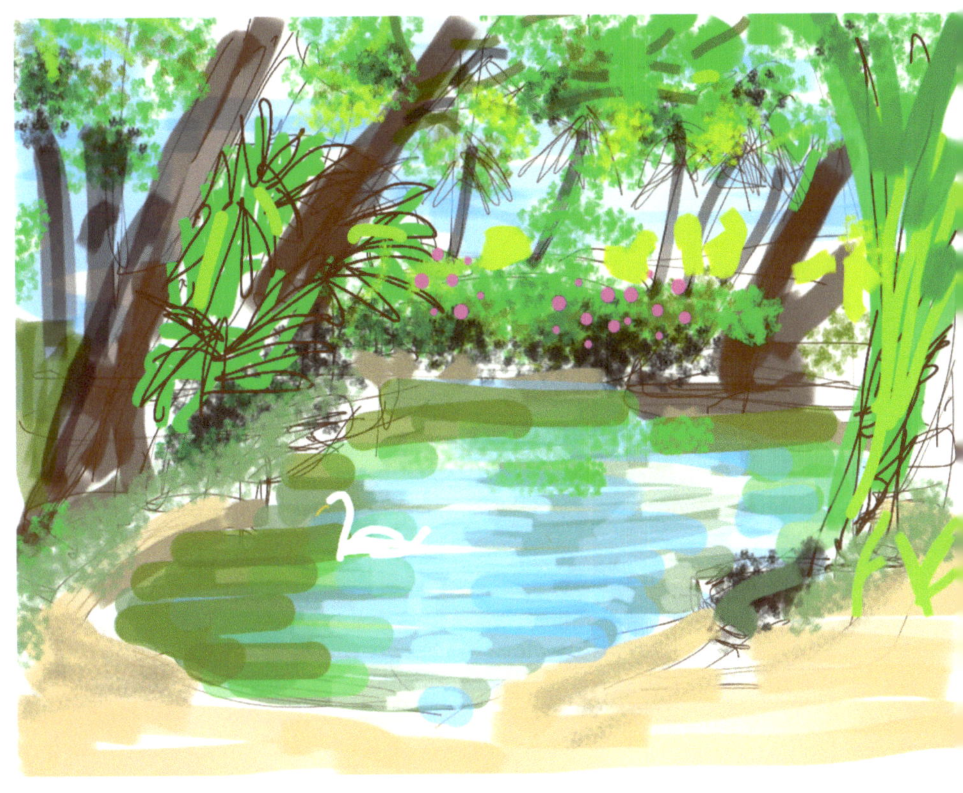

iPad Impressionist Sketching

With your iPad, you can produce a sketch using dabs of color the way color is used on an impressionist painting. At museums, the impressionist paintings look recognizable from a distance. When you look very closely, you notice they are made up of dabs of color, somewhat like the technique I used on the bottom picture of the opposite page.

Start by finding your perspective points and use your app's 2 px brush to electronically sketch in the line work as you see here.

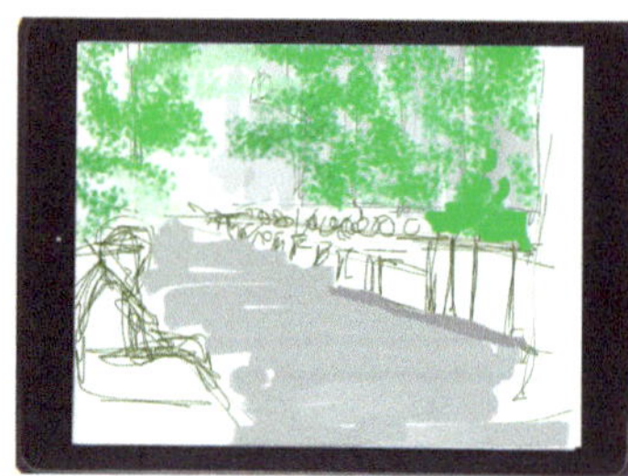

When you have developed your basic line layout, select another one of the app's electronic paintbrushes. The paintbrush size used for the drawing on the opposite page was 20 px.

Select colors from the app's color palette that relate to the scene that you are sketching, and dab the colors in their respective locations. Note how the colors are applied on the close-up shown on the bottom of the opposite page.

This sketch with my iPad was made at Union Square Park in New York City. It was a clear day in early fall and I was especially intrigued by the row of people sitting on park benches and the light and shadows that fell along the walkway. I sat on one of the benches and, with the exception of pigeon droppings from above, had a good and relaxing experience sketching there.

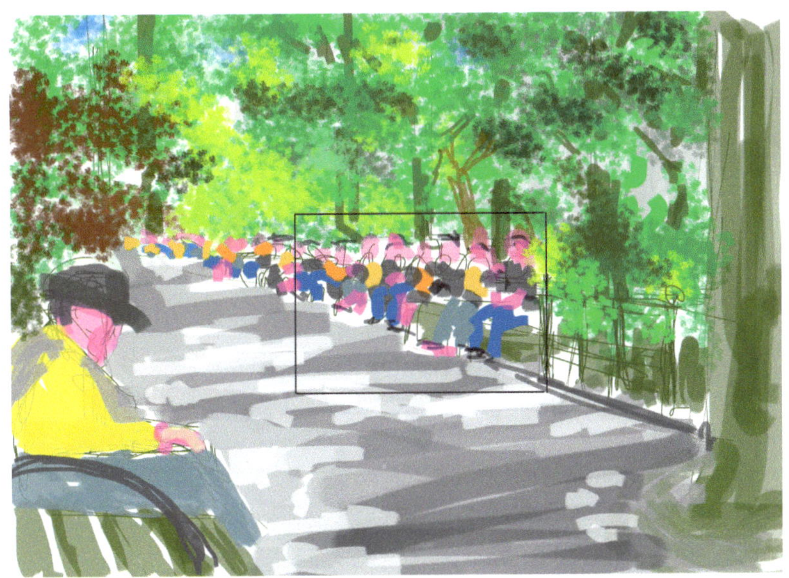

Rectangular area in the center is enlarged below

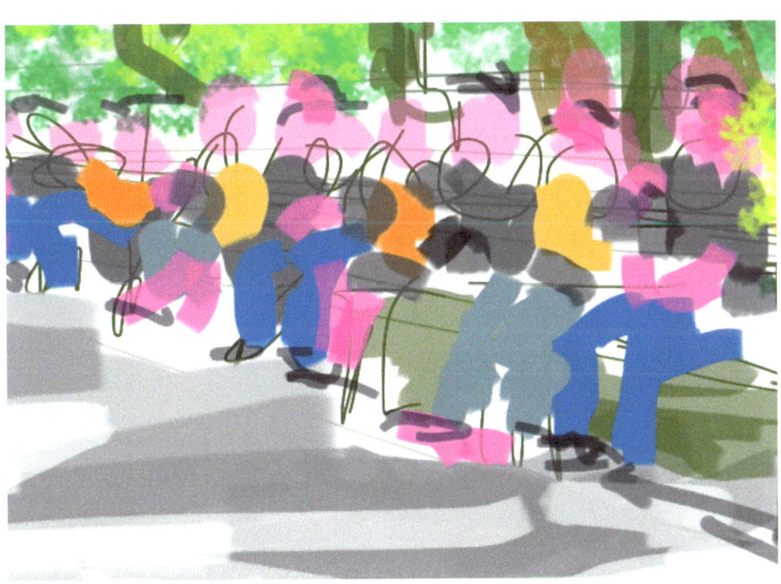

Close-up view of the sketch on top

Sketching Statues with the iPad

Paris is always a delight and there are so many sights to see and restaurants to discover that you must devote a portion of each day for sketching. While sightseeing at the remarkable Louvre, I was able to sit on a bench in the Tuileries Garden of the Louvre building and make a drawing at the park.

Also, while having lunch on a portico in the Louvre, I made this drawing from my lunch table, showing the statues along the wall as well as a small portion of The Louvre architecture. The sketch is a good reminder of my relaxing lunch there and a reminder of the wonderful things that the Louvre represents on the inside as well as the outside.

I sketched on the iPad by first laying out the perspective and forms of the statues, using a thin dark line, as you see here on this page.

When the elements were in position, I applied the color. The Ocher color for the statues was applied over the linework and different shades of Gray formed the clothing and figures of the statues.

Pale Yellow colored the Louvre structure on the right, with Grays for the windows and the terrace.

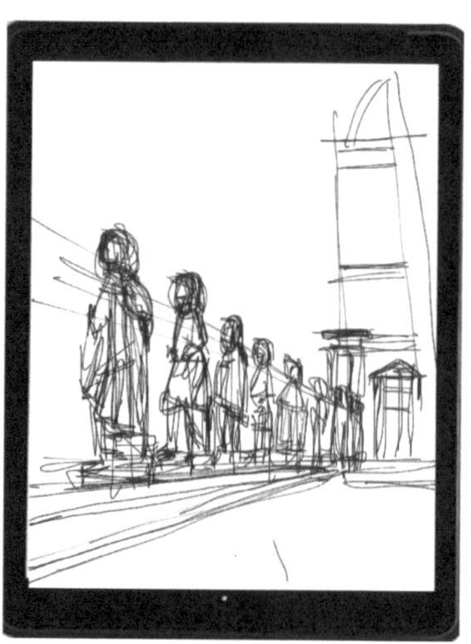

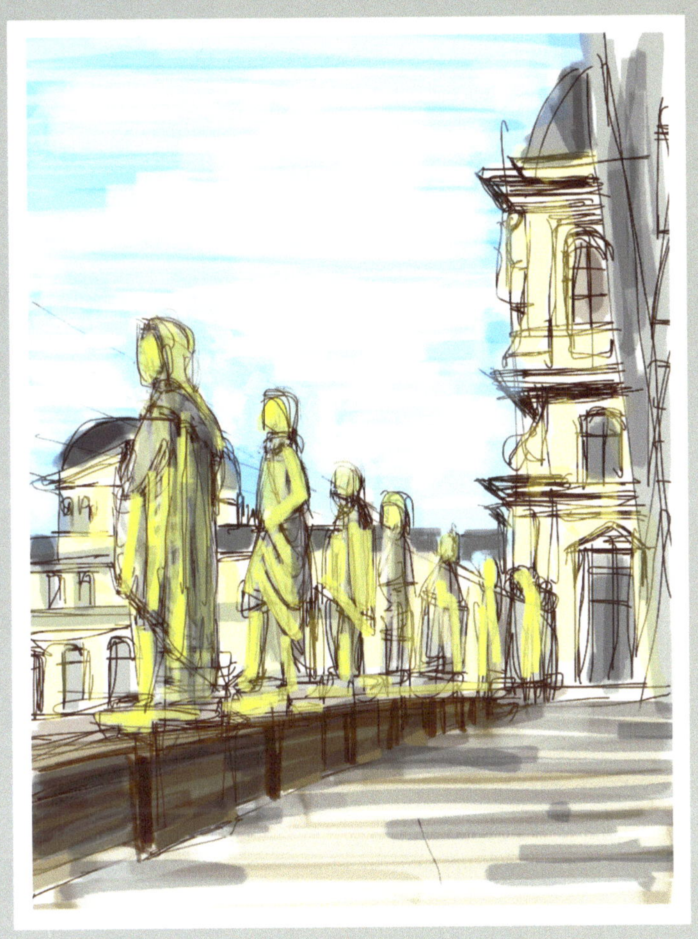

Albert Hall, Jaipur, India

Jaipur was probably my favorite city to visit in India because of its unique buildings, towers, hotels, palaces, and fascinating streets with every type of store imaginable. The streets are teaming with activity and what goes on within the streets are something rarely seen in any part of the world. For example, many streets have people selling food, flowers and other items, as well as passing cars, trucks, goats, camels, and even elephants. It is a wonderful city and there were things that constantly inspired me to make sketches on my iPad.

This particular drawing shows the Albert Hall, a museum in Jaipur. The main attraction of this museum is the building itself, with its beautifully elaborate Indo-Saracenic inspired domes, windows, and carved arches constructed from inlaid sand stone.

I found a place where I could sketch, which was among a large group of taxi drivers who were there to transport tourists. I was able to lean on a wall near where the drivers were parked and my sketching provided curiosity for the taxi drivers. They watched me carefully and a few who spoke English chatted briefly as to where I was from and other small talk. It looked like a palace, with many towers, balconies and arches making the building extremely interesting to sketch.

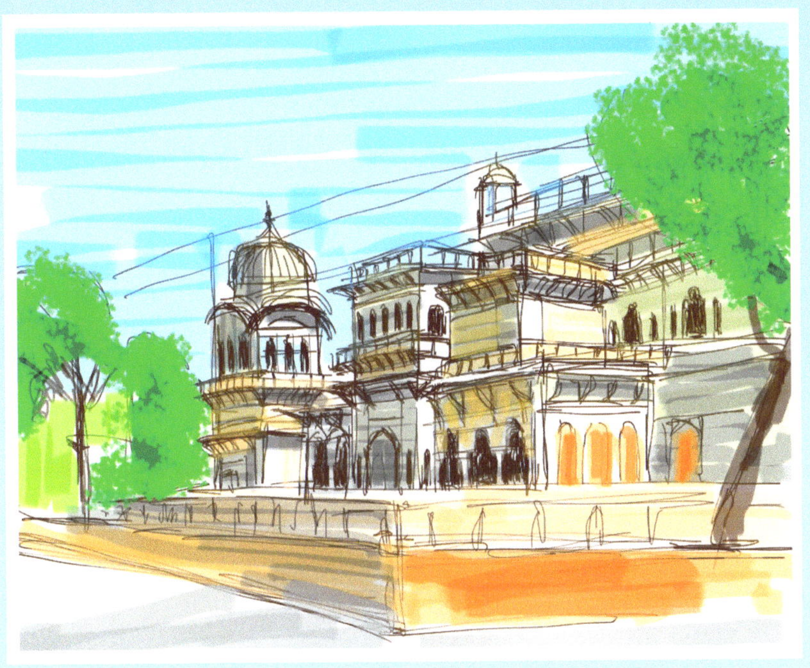

Water and Reflections

When traveling, I especially enjoy scenes on the water, since the water gives you the possibility of adding color and reflections that enhance your sketch. There are artists who are famous through their representation of water, and this often takes them years of experience and many hours, days or weeks to perfect each drawing.

In this book I recommend traveling from place to place spending efficient time on each sketch, so you can also go enjoy the next part of your travels. So keep your sketch strokes as simple as possible!

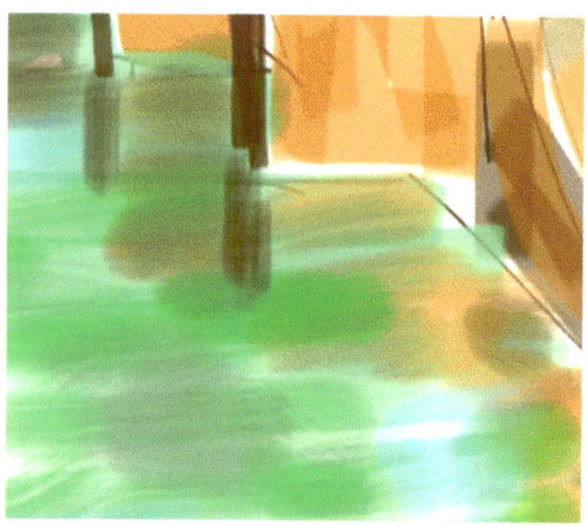 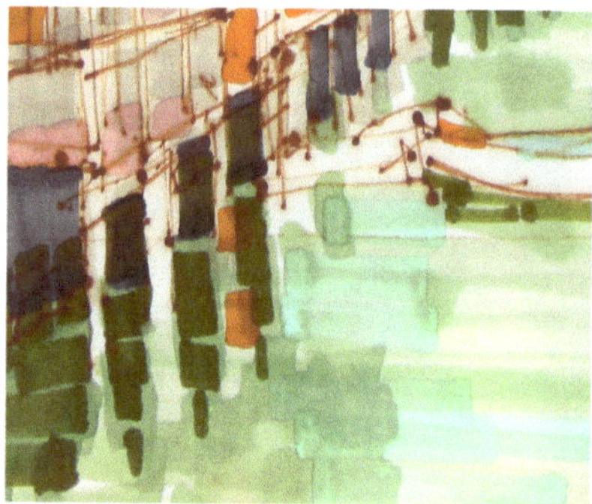

On the left is an iPad drawing and on the right is a Sketchpad/Marker drawing. The application of Willow Green – applied swiftly leaving spaces in between the strokes, makes a good color for the water surface on both drawings. Here I added a few strokes of Sapphire Blue over the Willow Green to reflect an element of the sky. The fun part of water sketching is adding the reflections from the objects on the shore. Bushes and trees will reflect Green color, buildings will usually reflect Gray, Brown, or Ocher colors, and other shore elements may also reflect in the water. Choose those colors for the water carefully from the shore colors that you have used, and add the reflections sparingly as you actually see them in the water.

The Thorbecke Square Canal is typical of many canals in Amsterdam, with boats docked on the side and archways in which the boats go through. This canal was surrounded by trees that formed an "overhanging roof" above it. I found a spot to place my iPad on the back of a bench facing the scene. The colors on the water reflect the trees and the structures on the sides.

Note the White spaces among paintstrkes on the water to suggest the combination of reflections and water ripples.

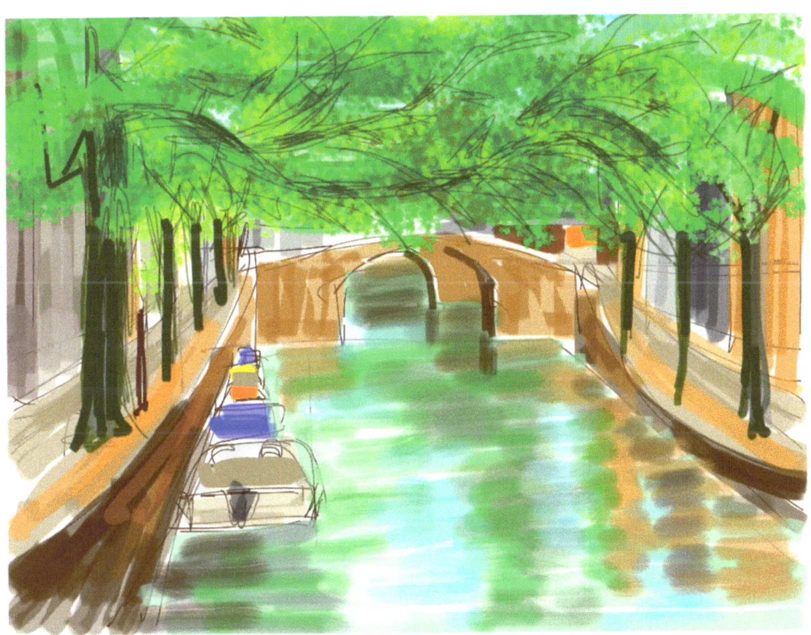

Sketching Water Reflections on the iPad

For sketching scenes with water, an hour with extremely clear weather will often give you the opportunity to get mirror-like reflections that enhance the drawing.

This sketch was made at a Vermont pond with my iPad. Note how the earlier part of the sketch, shown on this page, becomes enhanced when the tree reflections are added to the water (on the opposite page).

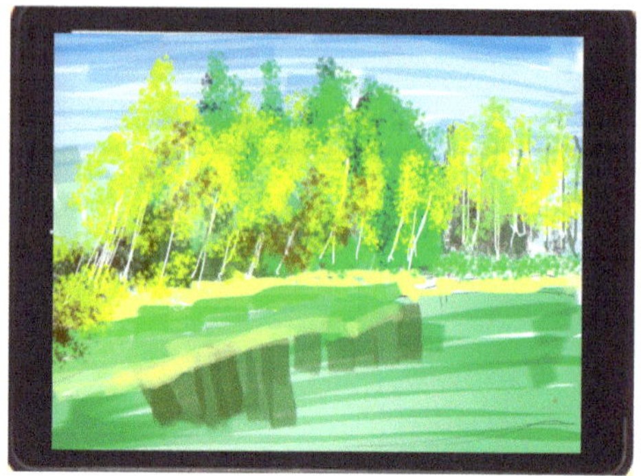

Toward the end of the month of October, I was strolling around a pond looking for colorful trees that might offer picturesque pond reflections. I was glad to see that the reflections actually mirrored the trees on the shore, with the exception of a few ripples. The trees reflecting in the water are slightly distorted on purpose, so that they appear to the viewer's eye to be rippling with the water. The ripples are formed by a few light paint strokes.

.

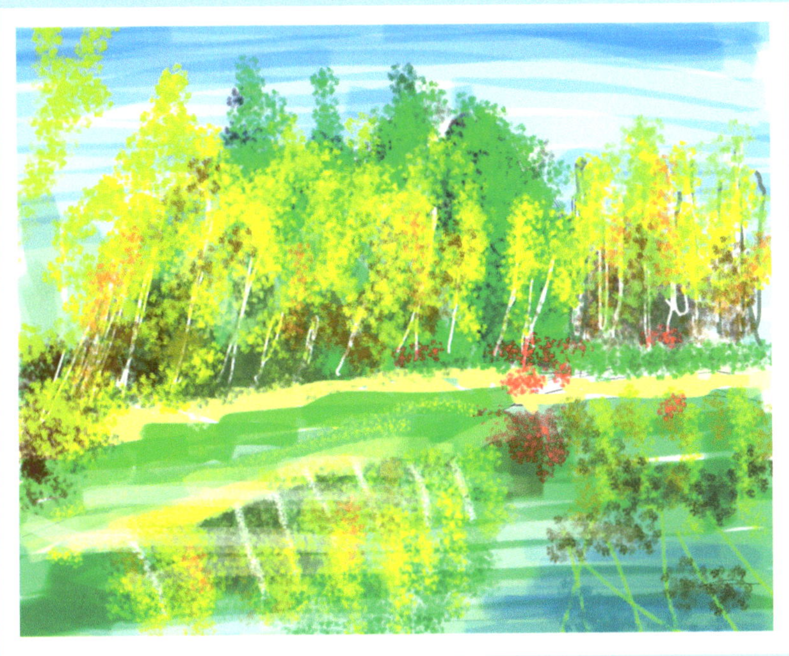

Nantucket Island, Massachusetts

Nantucket Island, off the coast of Massachusetts, is one of America's fine vacation spots for its combination of charming houses, boats, beaches, and the beauty of the town itself. We have spent many summers there and the summers are especially popular because of the breezes that always flow throughout the island. For years I have made drawings in different parts of Nantucket. There are many artists in Nantucket who travel there or live there in order to take advantage of its surroundings and the beauty of its nature, houses and waterways.

This is from a series of drawings that I made through the years. When I pass these locations I remember the enjoyment of sketching and thinking about what those structures were used for. Some of the old structures themselves have remained for hundreds of years, and the entire island of Nantucket is considered an historic district. This limits the changes that can be made on the island without approval from a landmark commission that is part of the town structure.

This sketch shows a 1-point perspective view of a typical Nantucket Island wharf. I sat on the dock with my drawing pad and markers to try to capture the essence of the scene. The 1-point perspective with its vanishing point in the background emphasizes the depth of field. The combination of the pilings, houses, and water reflections add interest to Nantucket's soft colors. It's important along with the recessive colors such as Blue, Green, and Gray, to add a warm color – the warmer Orange and Yellow colors enliven the sketch -- so I will use the Yellow and the Orange to vitalize the scene. Some artists don't take advantage of the warmer colors on a drawing, but to me they are important in making the drawing come to life!

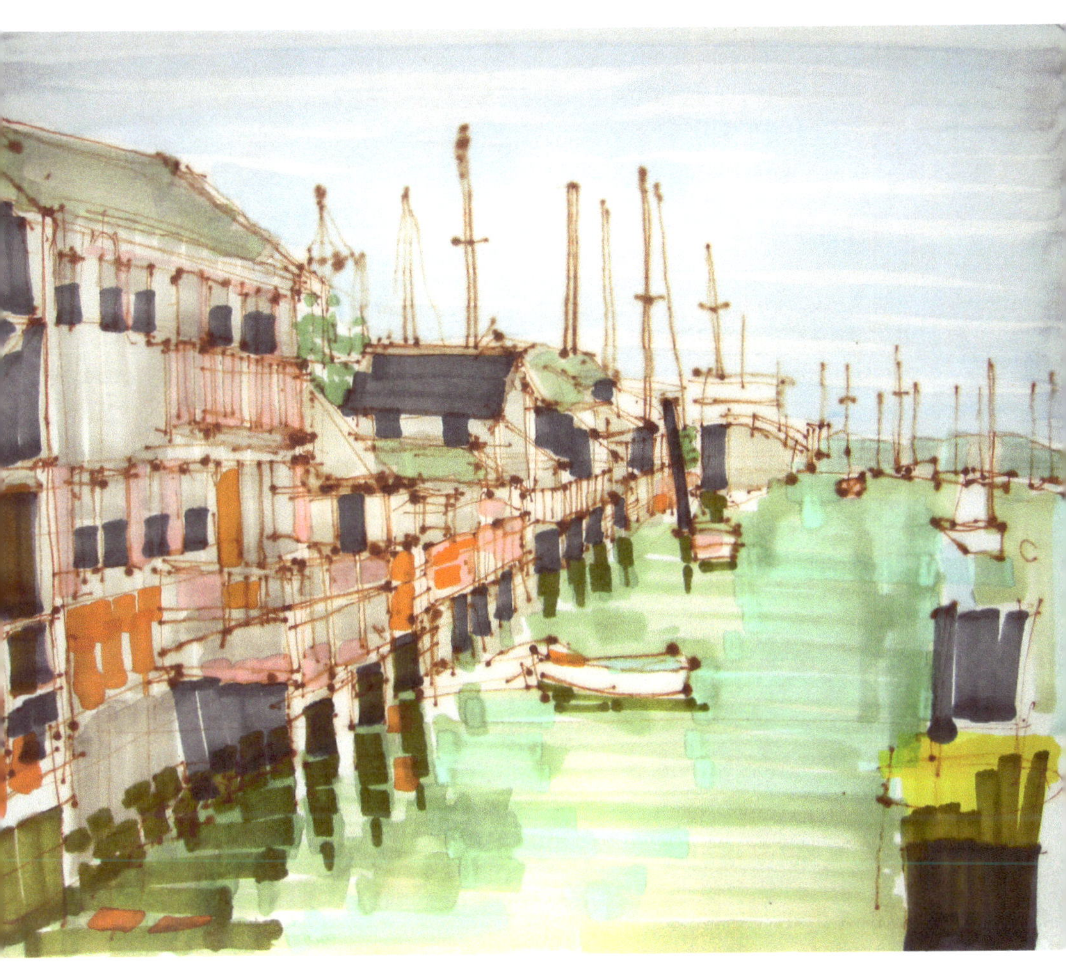

Swain's Wharf, Nantucket

In Nantucket, Massachusetts, I was fascinated by the way this group of houses were built very close together on pilings and created the look of a miniature town. Most of the houses on Swain's Wharf are quite small and, while drawing them, one can imagine the interesting people who inhabit the houses. As I sat on the wharf and made the drawing, I concentrated heavily on the perspective and the depth needed to make the houses visually separate from one another.

It was important to capture the shadows under the houses in the reflections in the water, in order to make the houses look like they appeared above the water on their pilings.

As with other houses in Nantucket, the shingles on all surfaces were Gray and in order to give extra life to the drawing, I added some warm Orange and Pink to contrast with the Gray color of the houses.

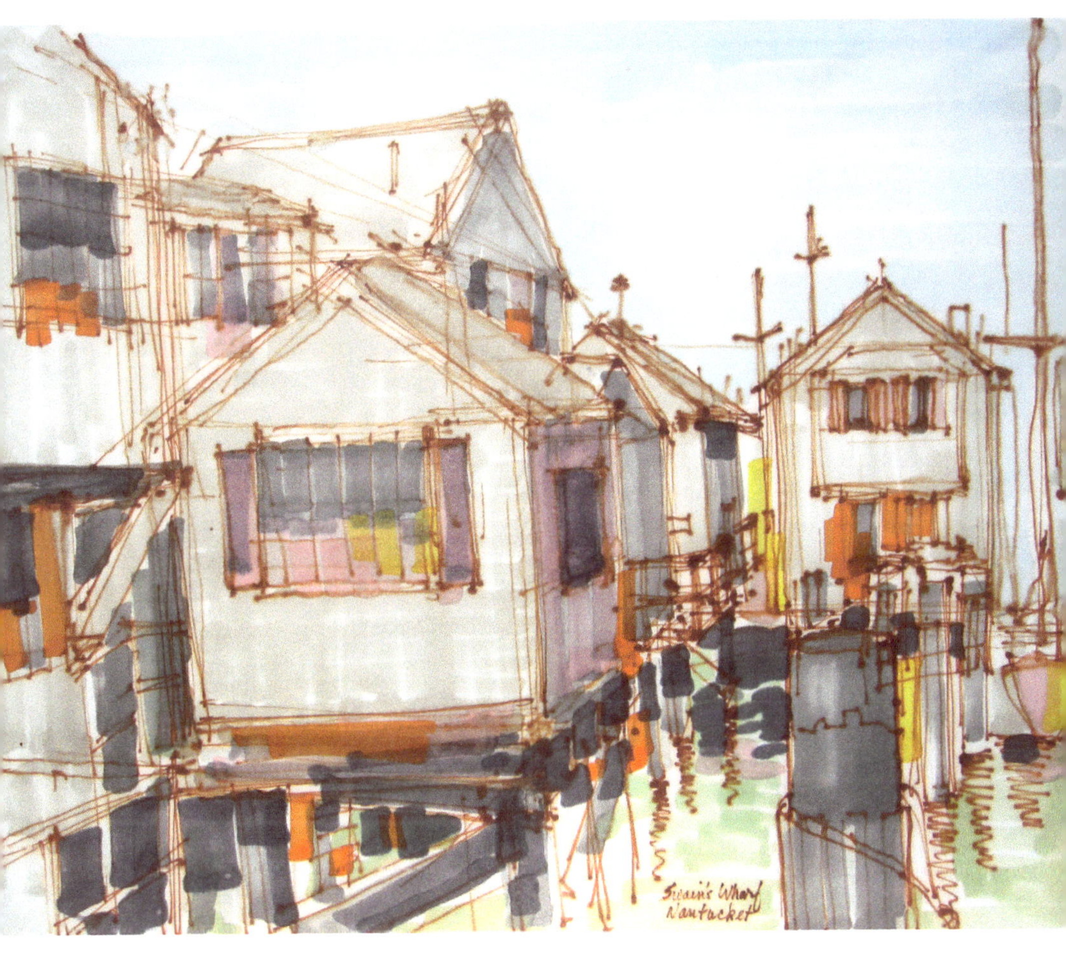

61

Nantucket Harbor

Steamboat Wharf in Nantucket is the pier from which the main steamship embarks and returns from Hyannis, Massachusetts. While sitting on this wharf, I was fascinated by the combination of the large, orange freighter with the small gray houses. As with many of the wharf houses, being raised above the water on pilings creates interesting shadows and reflections. I kept this drawing purposely sketchy so that one could concentrate on the color patterns and not be distracted by specific details.

The Brant Point Lighthouse is a symbol of Nantucket, placed on the beach at the harbor for the main part of the town. Every vessel traveling across Nantucket Sound will pass the Brant Point Lighthouse before landing in a harbor in Nantucket. As an island icon, it is probably one of the most photographed places on Nantucket.

Through the experience of drawing the Lighthouse, I was able to concentrate on its proportions and its tower, railings and proximity to the Sound that make up its architecture. It is surrounded by foliage, beach-fencing and rocks, and it was important for me to get the general feeling without specifically showing every detail.

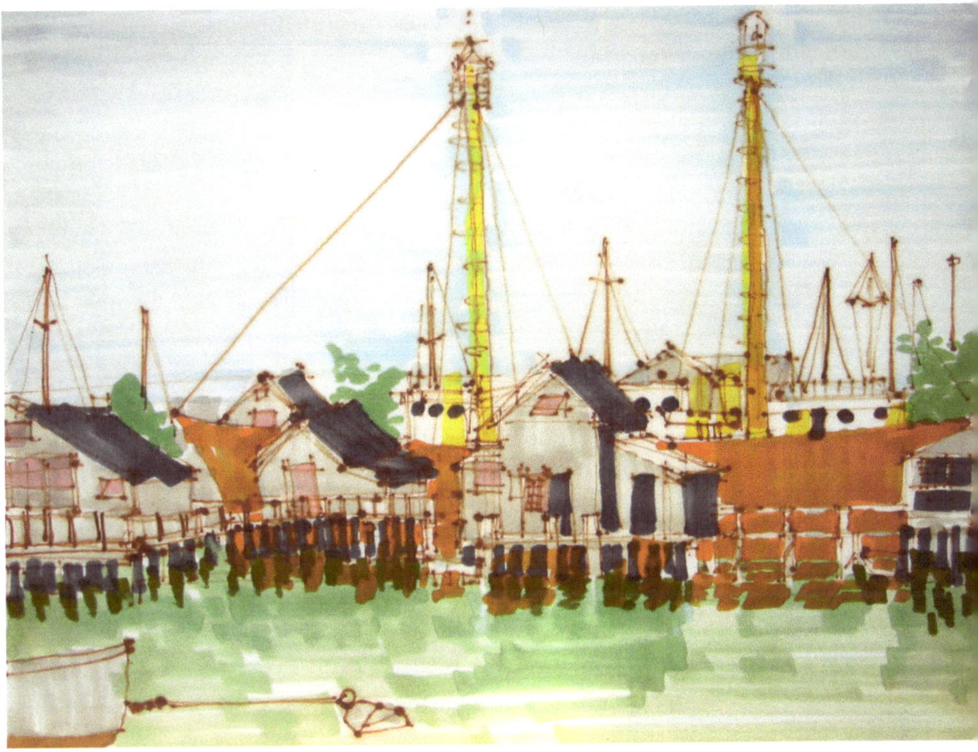

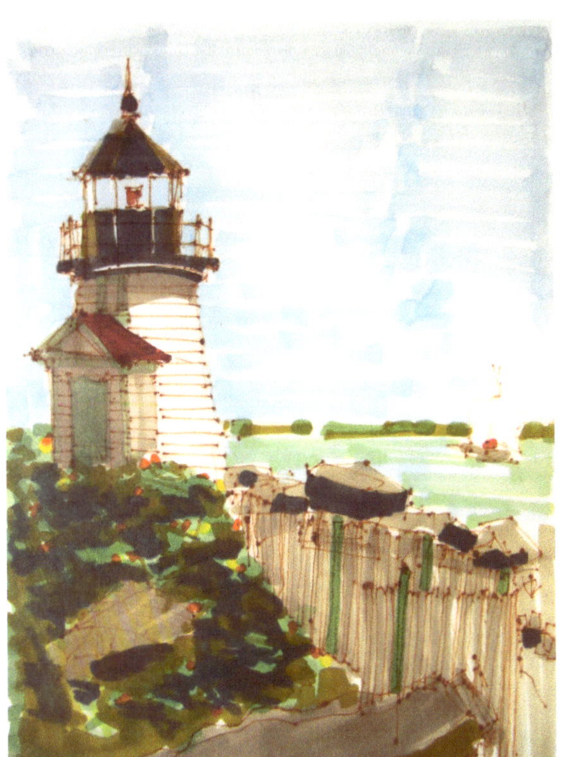

Floating Village, Cambodia

This unique scene was about 1 1/2 hours from Siem Reap in Cambodia. All of the houses were actually in the water, giving this region the name, "Floating Village".

I refer to this drawing as my "moving target," since the boats in the foreground kept moving and shifting with the tide. For this drawing I was also sitting on a boat, so my boat was moving one way, while the other boats were not in unison. I had to work quickly and keep in mind what the boats look like when they were in certain positions. As a further challenge, the light was changing and other boats with people were moving around. I spent two hours on my boat swaying and sketching and trying to get a feeling for the colors and the houses that surround the scene.

I think the most memorable thing about making this drawing was my watching the changes that occurred --- with people moving in and out of the floating houses, taking boats back and forth from the floating houses and the activity that occurs within this particular part of the world.

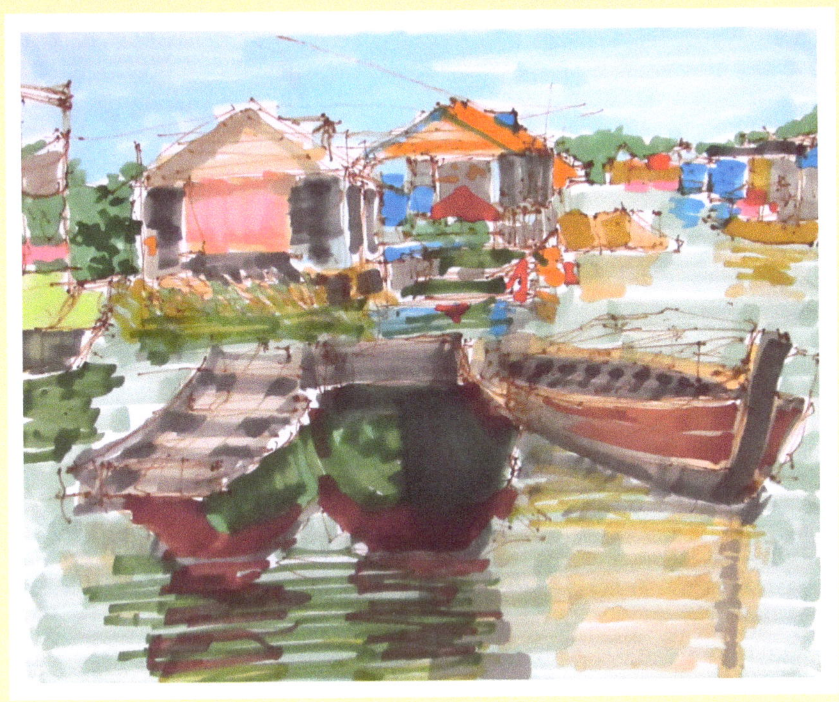

Tran Quac Pagota, Vietnam

This is a well-known part of a park near Hanoi, Vietnam called the Tran Quac Pagoda. It is certainly reminiscent of pagoda structures in this part of the world, and I was especially fascinated by the pagoda's pinkish color, the outlying ocher-colored buildings, the palm trees, and their reflections in the water.

It happened that there were about 15 to 20 Vietnamese art students drawing the same scene. However, when I sat down near them and started my drawing, they stopped their own drawing and walked over to watch what I was doing. I presume it was the unusual scene of an older man making a drawing and, in their minds, having the experience through the years of doing this type of work. They watched me intently and gathered around me. In fact at times some of them stood in front of me so that I actually had to politely ask them to move so I could still see what I was drawing. Very few words were exchanged although one or two of the students that spoke English did ask where I was from and then kept watching what I was doing. It was nice to know that the students were perhaps learning the sketching technique by watching me.

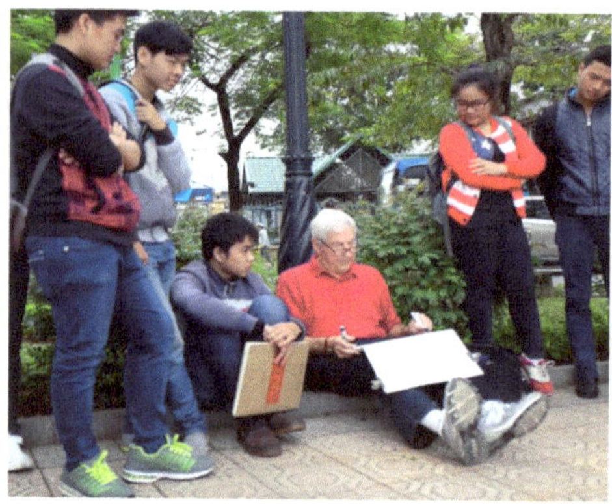

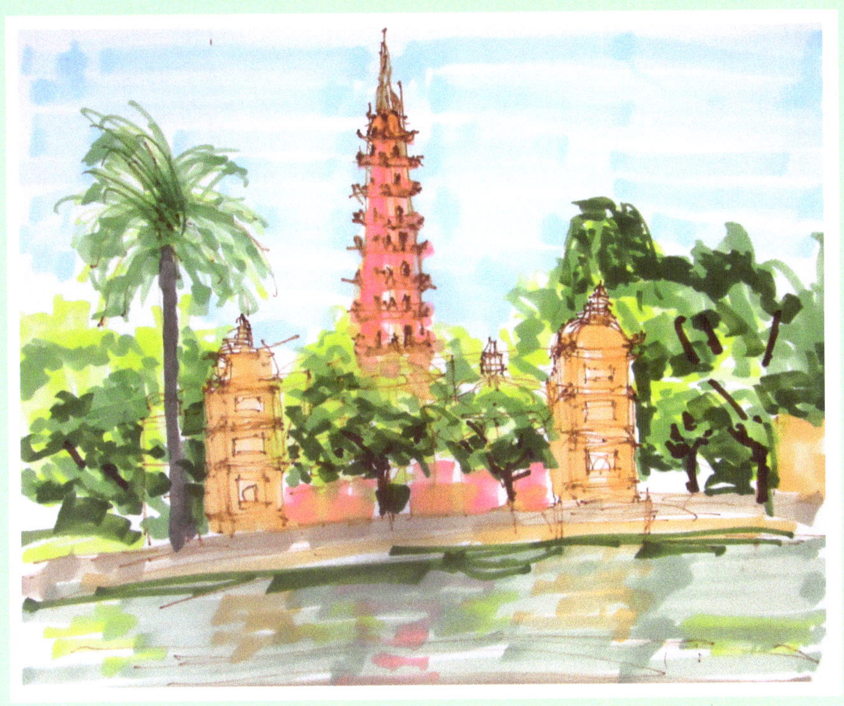

Hoi An, Vietnam

Hoi An, one of my favorite cities in Vietnam, is located in the central south region. It is an unusual shopping town, since there are stores ranging from very upscale down to low-end discount shops. Many tourists come to this town for shopping experiences, and the town has some interesting architecture, parks and restaurants. I had a good shopping experience there, since I found a store in which the young owners design jewelry, and I was able to pick out some wonderful gifts for my family at very reasonable prices.

While walking around the area I discovered a part that would be interesting to draw called the Japanese Bridge. The architecture of this bridge was fascinating and within the bridge were restaurants and stores. I walked around the pond that flowed under the bridge, passing many tourists and tables and I found a chair in a café where I could sit and sketch.

As I was unloading the drawing pad and the markers, a family was sitting at the next table and their little girl came over to watch what I was doing. I started drawing the scene and the little girl spent the time sitting at one of the chairs at my table and carefully surveying my art equipment, playing with each of the markers, and thoroughly observing what I was doing for a full hour. She didn't say a word but she kept very busy and was sorting my markers as though they were toys. Since she was so interested, this didn't bother me and I felt like it was only adding to my own fine experience to feel that she was learning something by observing.

The scenery was quite unique with the open houses in the background and this very unusual bridge structure in the foreground. The roof of the structure, the materials, the columns and the way the structure reflected in the pond all added to this scene. And the memory of this little girl's enjoyment and interest in the art that I was doing also added to the pleasure of my being there.

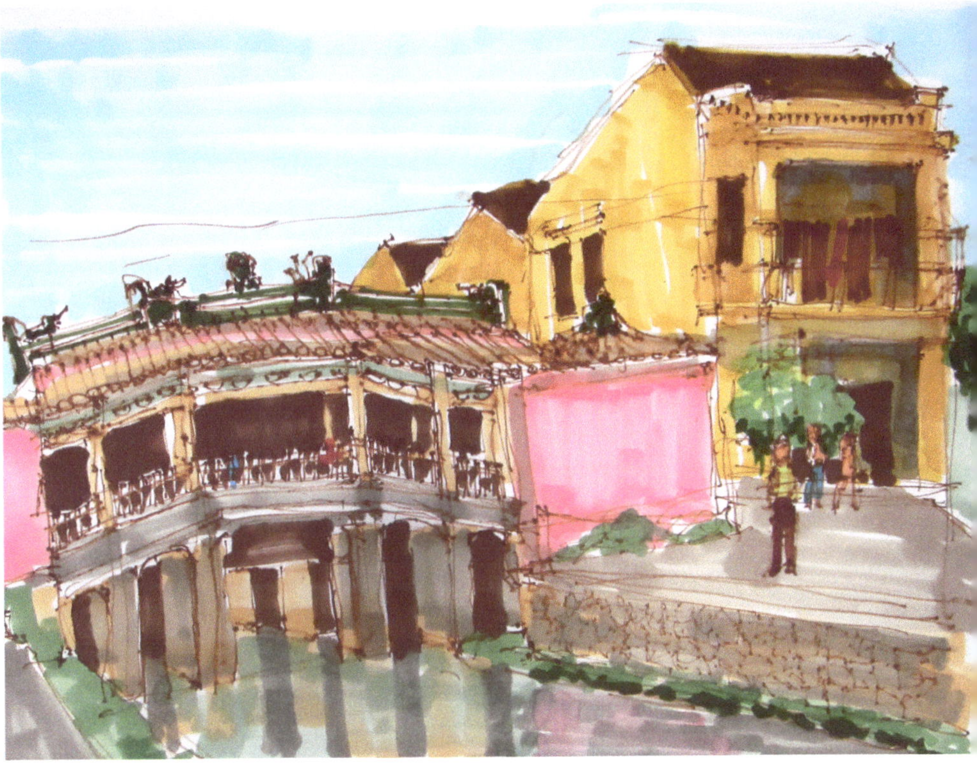

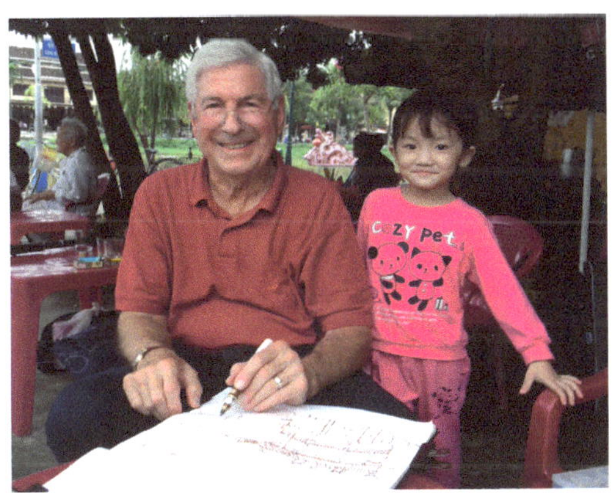

Houseboats in Hong Kong

The houseboats reveal life itself. By sitting on the shore and drawing these houseboats, I was able to view families living, talking, dining, washing clothes and everything that goes on in one's daily routine of life. I was able to concentrate on the shape of the boats and the way they hug the water and sit side-by-side.

I was able to watch schoolchildren leave their houseboat to go to school on shore by taking a smaller size dinghy and sliding it along a rope line from the houseboat to the shore. (Note the ropelines in the drawing.) And these children were young – as young as six and seven years old, headed for school on their own. They knew how to commandeer the little boats that took them to shore. Although the adults in the houseboats were dressed in work clothes and showed signs of poverty, the children were dressed in finery – clean blouses, trousers, skirts and whatever it took to make them look totally clean and prepared for their studies.

It was a wonderful sight to watch, and very worthwhile making the drawing, seeing the way the children anticipated going to school, with circumstances that would be difficult for any family. So I have many memories from this particular drawing.

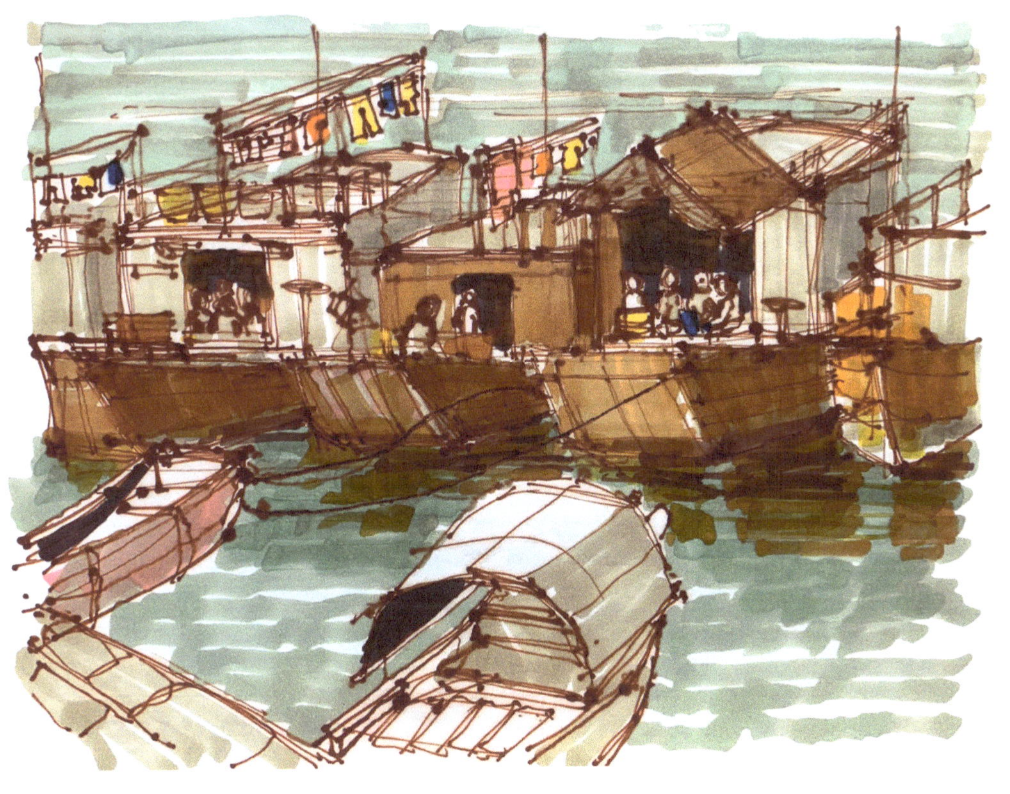

Villa Carlotta, Italy

For wonderful water scenery, take a trip to Lake Como in the northern part of Italy, an hour in driving distance from Milan. Surrounding Lake Como are many beautiful towns where you can tour and never run out of interesting places to sketch. I had a rented car at the time and traveled to some of the surrounding towns by car, some by bus, and some by ferry boat.

I took a ferry from our hotel to a village on Lake Como called Villa Carlotta, made up of walkways, hillsides, and wonderful floral and landscape arrangements. One can walk around Villa Carlotta's gardens and see its art masterpieces and villa surrounded by lake and mountains. I spent several hours walking around this area.

Toward the end of the day, while standing on the platform waiting for the ferry to go back to our hotel, I found this charming scene. I took out my drawing pad and, with the water in the foreground and mountains in the background did a sketch of Villa Carlotta as it appears by the lake. I found this to be a wonderful way to spend time waiting for the ferry and a way to capture the colors and the charm of this part of Lake Como.

The marker colors used for the sketch (over the Brown line layout) are Willow Green on the water and mountains, Grass Green and Olive Green on the trees, Light Sand on the buildings and water reflections, Celery color on some trees and mountains, Banana color on mountains, Saphire Blue on sky and water reflections, and Warm Grays 4 and 7.

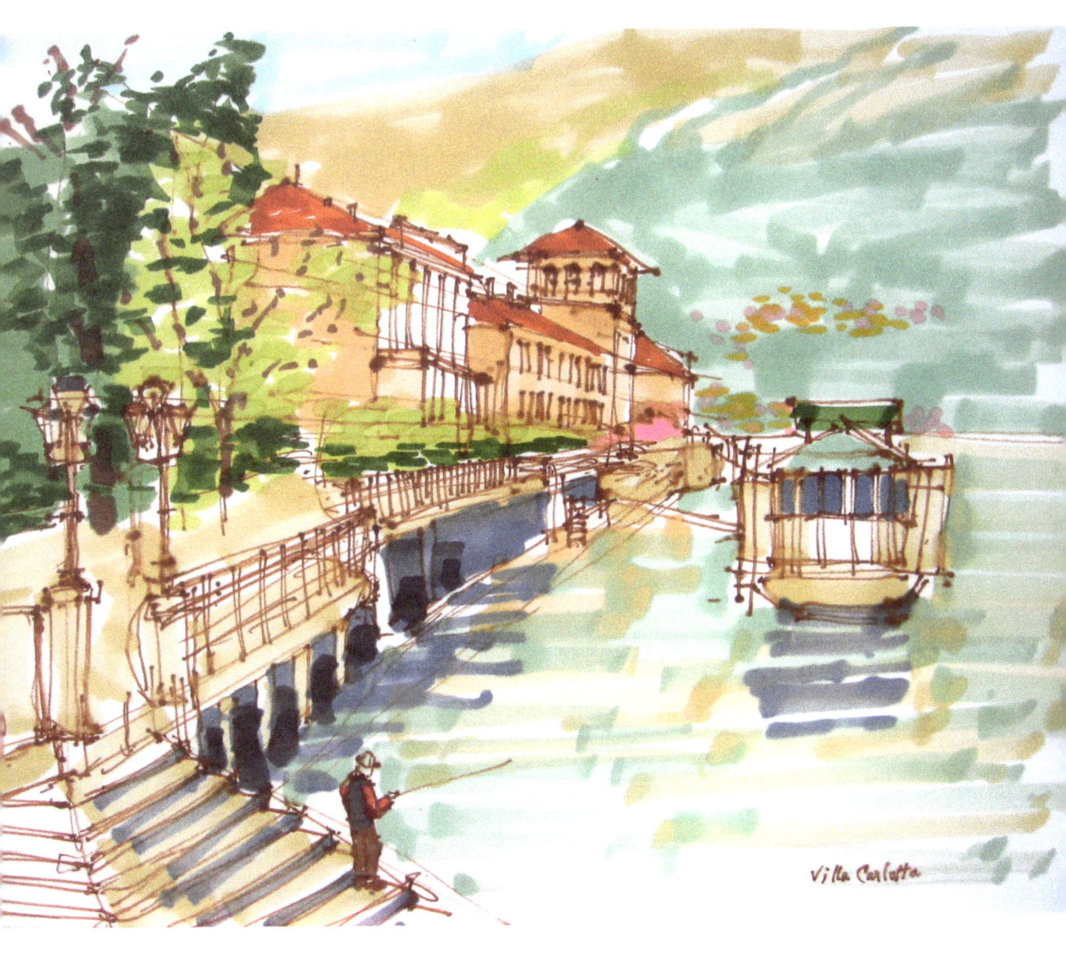
Villa Carlotta

Thames Path near Hampton Court, UK

Traveling to London is always a treat, since there is so much going on within the city and its outskirts. For sketching, I especially enjoy some of the suburban areas surrounding London, and strolling around there will give you the opportunity to explore these charming towns and villages.

This area on the shore of the Thames River -- called "Thames Path" -- was near Hampton Court. The scenery was beautiful with the combination of seaways, boats and tudor style row houses, and I found a bridge on which to get a view of all this for sketching. In fact, the row houses reminded me of some of the homes from where I grew up in Forest Hills, New York, at which a certain section was built in the English Tudor style. I remember from my youth that photos of houses in England looked similar to these Tudor style houses, so it was especially delightful for me to stand on the bridge and make the sketch of the houses. As usual, I try to find a place to sketch and rest my drawing pad, and found a side wall that was part of the bridge structure. The combination of houses, trees, shrubbery, waterway and small boats came together to make it interesting for me, and I was able to study the elements closely.

For the water, colors are Willow Green, Grass Green, Warm Grey 2, and Olive.

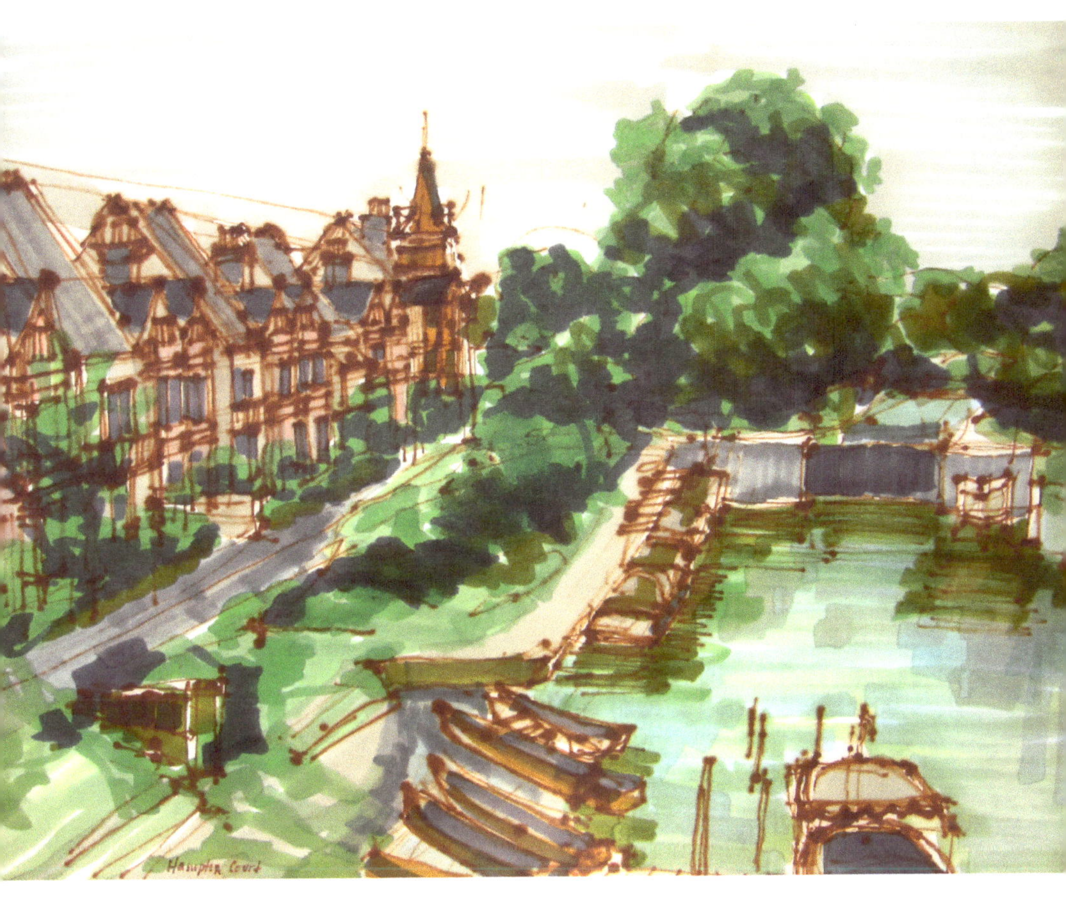

Hampton Court

Cassis, France

Cassis is a small seaside resort on the Mediterranean Sea not far from the city of Marseilles. It's a charming town with excellent sea views and a wonderful place to stroll, with its picturesque fishing port, cafés and restaurants.

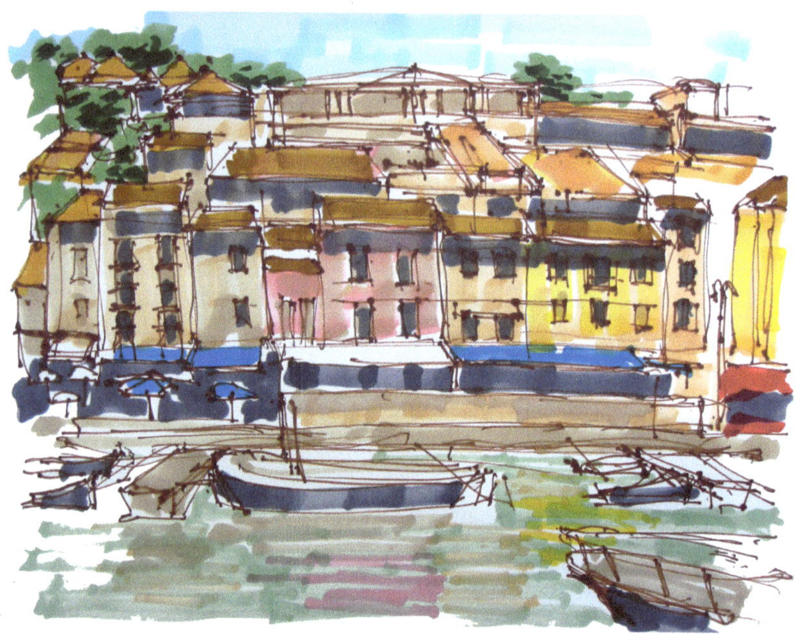

Walking past part of the beach and looking down towards an area of charming buildings, I saw a scene to sketch. Among the colorful buildings were several outdoor cafés and small boats. I set up my drawing pad on a tall trash can near the water, across from these colorful buildings. I like the act of sketching to be spontaneous – pull out the pad, pull out the markers and go for it!

When the boats, trees or buildings are colorful, the reflections in the water will add interest to your drawing. Here, the building colors were part of the character of the village, and their reflections appear in the water. You can see the perspective of the picture used a vanishing point above the roofs of the structures. The reflections react to the stillness or roughness of the water, and enliven the sketch.

Bellagio, Italy

Bellagio is probably the most popular town on Lake Como for tourists. Its beauty is derived from the waterfront with picturesque structures, old hotels, and the mountains that rise around the town to form a combination that delights everybody.

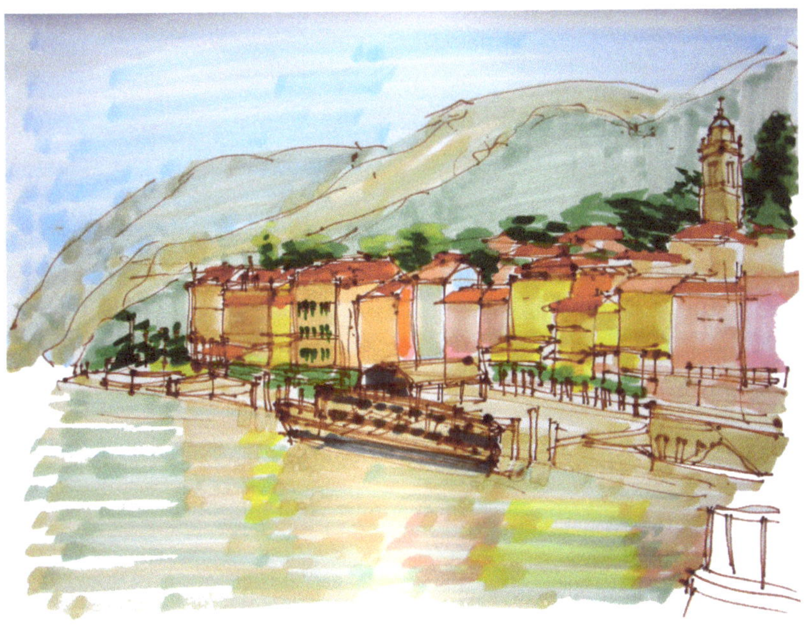

I wanted to capture the feeling of the colorful houses in Bellagio reflecting in the water, and also the subtlety of the mountains in the background. So I strolled for a while along a walkway and a bridge until I found a spot on the bridge that would be a good vantage point for sketching. It's always worth taking the time to find the right spot for sketching, and sometimes finding that spot becomes a challenge. I placed my sketchpad on a wall in front of the bridge, layed out the drawing with thin line, and added the colors of the houses.

The water reflects the colors of the mountains and the houses along the shore. The boat in the foreground is a taxi boat that takes mostly tourists around to the different towns in Lake Como, with Bellagio an important destination.

Sketching Flowers

Nothing brightens up a drawing like flowers. You have the opportunity to make your sketch look especially colorful and enlightening with the use of flowers. When traveling, I am often attracted to a scene such as a flower market or a building with flowers around it. I know that this scene will give me the opportunity to make a drawing that will be eye-catching.

 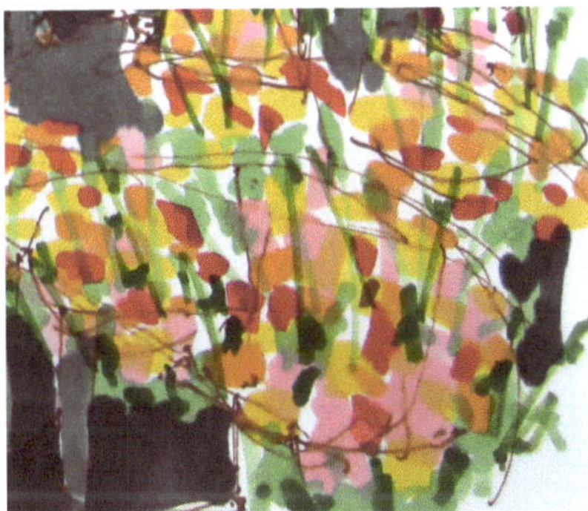

As I've said before, the key to sketching when traveling is to keep it simple. After you have sketched your basic layout, pick out the colors of the flowers that are in front of you and use those colors just to make dots of color on your drawing. To save time, you do not need specific flower shapes, since the flower areas should be sketchy. Note the simplicity of the flower strokes on the iPad drawing (above left) and the Sketchpad/Marker drawing (above right).

With each of the following drawings, the flowers became a strong and decorative element. You will note that the sketchiness of the flowers enabled me to save time and complete the drawing quickly and efficiently.

Sketching Flowers in Jaipur, India

India is a country unlike any place that most westerners have seen. The second most populated country in the world, India is colorful, chaotic and spectacular – a real challenge for artists!

When walking around Jaipur, India, I thought this flower market was a striking scene. The coloration was bright and the men's clothing consisted of bright colors. I used my iPad for a perspective view that would emphasize the colorful rows of flowers and the men's clothing. The overall effect is a perspective that takes the viewer's eye though the vibrant color scene, with dabs of color used to represent the flowers.

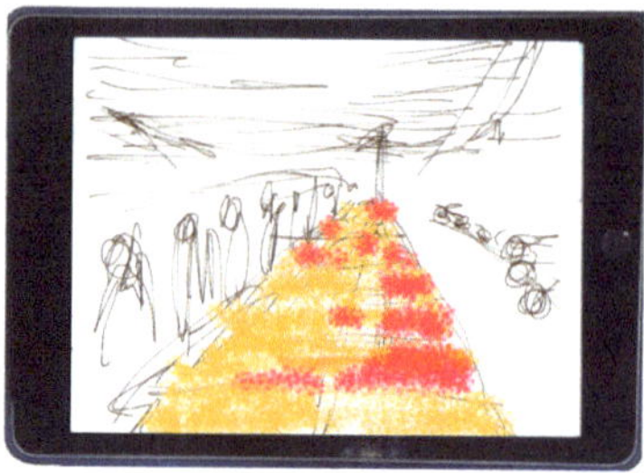

Starting iPad layout...

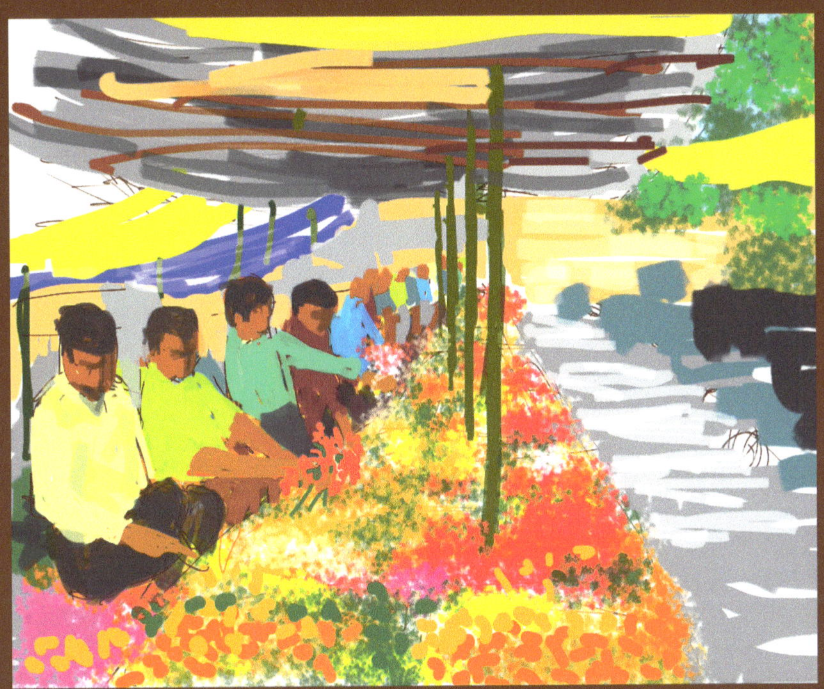

Final iPad sketch

Aix-en-Provence, France

I was carrying my art supplies through the winding streets of Aix-en-Provence, France, thinking that perhaps I would see something on the spot to sketch. As soon as I saw the numerous flower markets, I realized that they would be excellent places to draw.

This drawing was made at my favorite flower market in the town of Aix, and near this market were many vendors selling clothing, food, spices and jewelry. The flower market was filled with residents and visitors and was surrounded by trees and café tables. One Sunday morning I walked over there from the apartment that we had rented, and found among the many tables one empty café table where I felt it would be convenient to sketch. In order not to lose my seat, I ordered a demitasse of coffee like many of the other people there.

I took out my sketchpad and markers and started to sketch the flower market, using the umbrellas as a colorful way to provide depth for the sketch.

When you travel to a location to sketch, it is advantageous to find a seat, and even better a table and chair near the area that you want to draw. This enables you to conveniently layout your materials and relax while you are making the drawing. Of course, you are especially lucky if the view from the seat happens to have a clear view of what you wish to draw.

There were tables that were in front of me (which I left out of the drawing) in which people were sitting, so there was some interference with my view. But yet I could look around those people and get the view that I wanted. As with any drawing of this sort, there were people moving in and out, buying flowers, and standing around making conversation. It was relaxing to be sitting at a nice table and enjoying the view and the busy movements of people selling flowers, buying flowers, cutting flowers and putting together bunches for the many people shopping there.

The one figure that was permanent was the man sorting out the flowers. I decided that I would use him in the drawing for size and interest, and leave out all of the people who were moving in and out, especially since the flowers and the umbrellas offered so much interest and color to the drawing. I framed out the drawing with my pointed marker and once I had achieved my basic layout, I started filling in the colors.

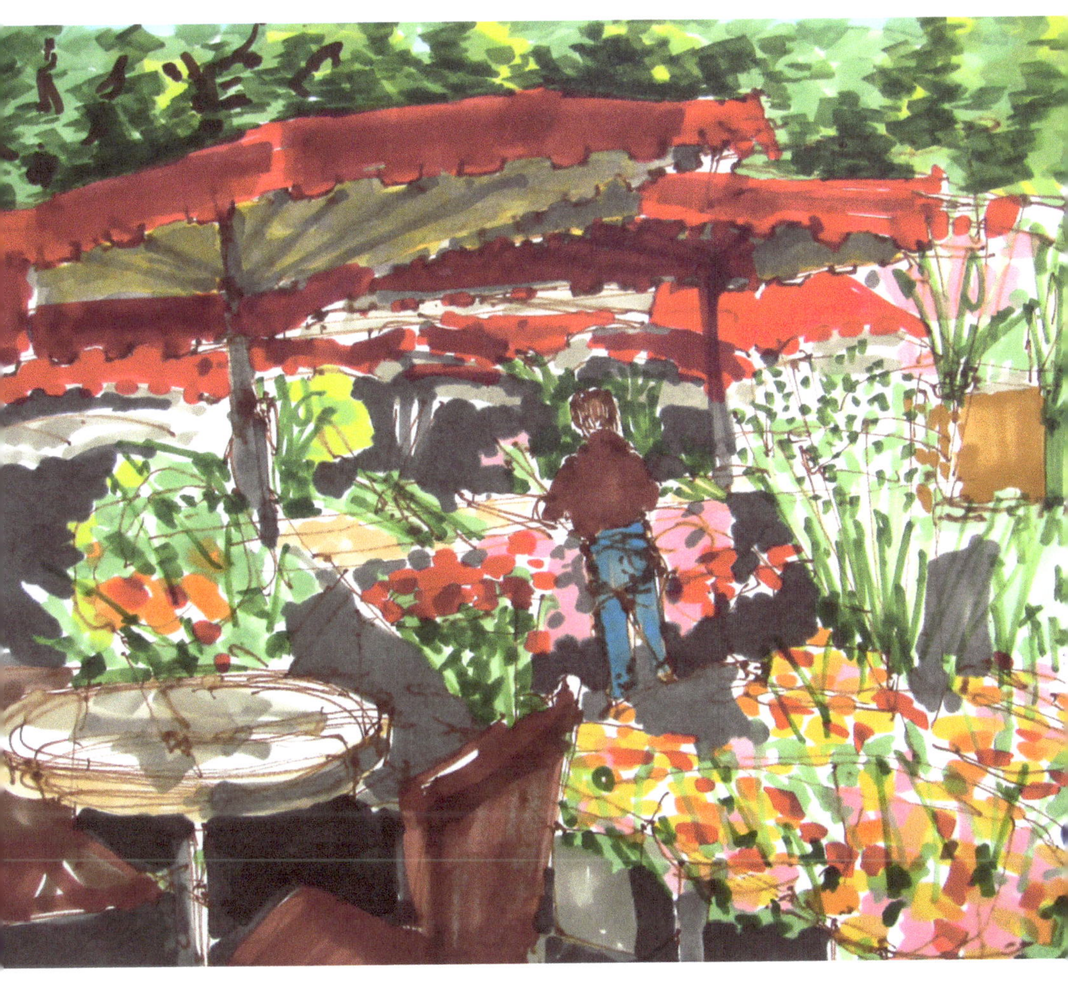

The Big Foreground

A good way to give dimension to your drawing is by using a large foreground object. For example, in a drawing on my earlier chapter on perspective, I showed a statue of a lion in the foreground, which gave strong dimension to the Parliament Building scene. During your travels, statues can frequently be used as foreground objects, since they are often placed in front of structures or monuments. I try to take advantage of scenes using statues, boats, fences, or waterfront pilings in the foreground.

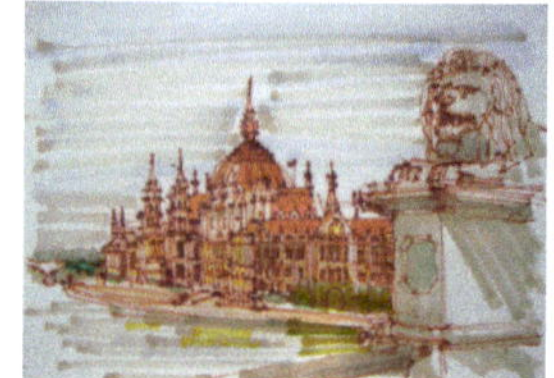

When drawing these foreground objects, their proportion to the subject in the drawing does not have to be 100% accurate – use your "artistic license" to enable the foreground object to fit on your paper while contrasting in size to the elements placed behind it. On some of my drawings, the foreground object was close to me so that it would have appeared much larger than shown in my drawing. So I purposely drew a foreground size relationship that fit well on the paper along with the architectural subject in the background.

On the opposite page, these vessels in the foreground give dimension to the sketch and give the viewer a sense of the size of the area encompassed by the drawing. To enliven the sketch, I used the bright yellow color of the boat to contrast with the tan beach sand and the wood color of the dune fencing. This scene is a beachfront at Smith's Point at the most southwestern end of Nantucket Island.

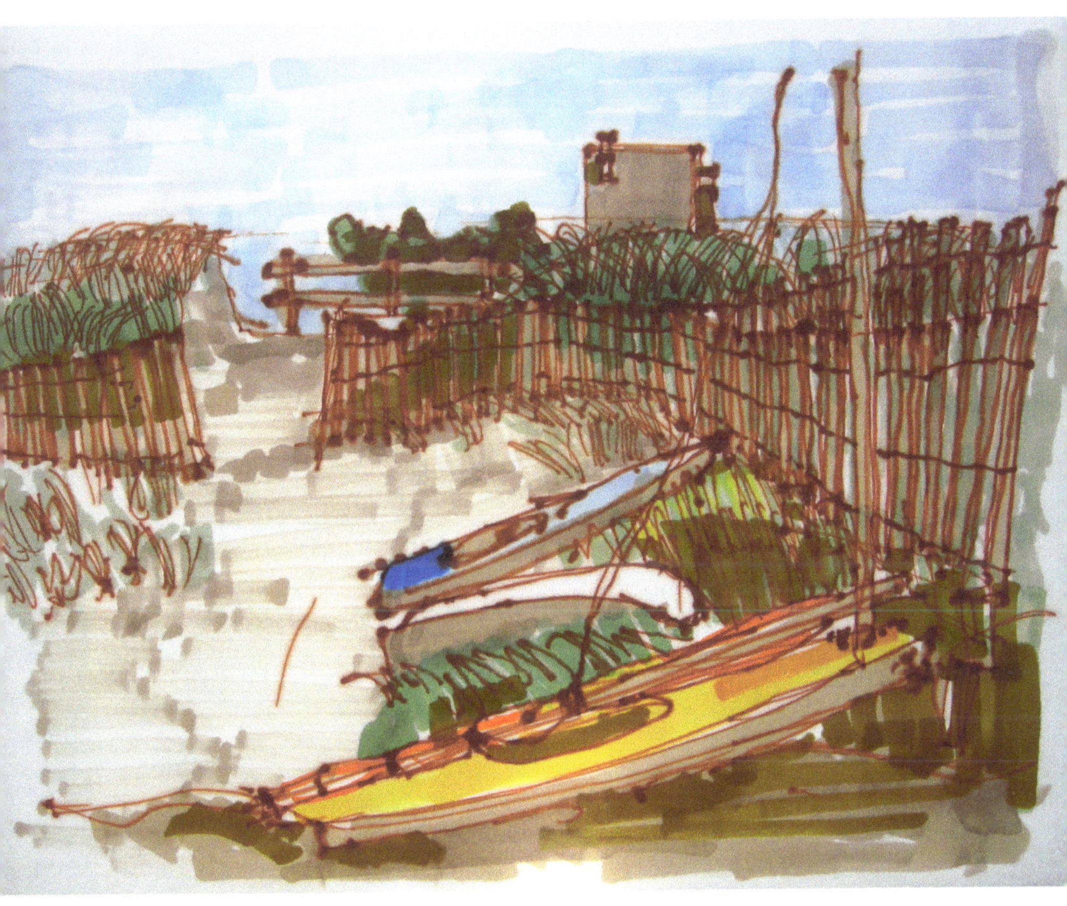

The Big Foregriund Statue

A large foreground object is an important part of each of the sketches in this chapter. These foreground objects not only add dimension to the sketches, but also add the elements of location and history.

For big foreground objects such as statues, first outline their position on your paper so that you know the object will fit comfortably with the rest of your sketch.

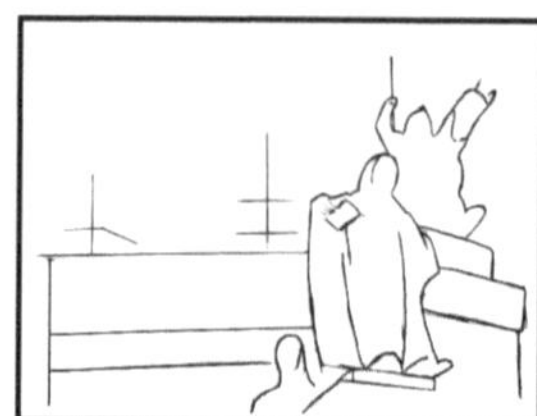

Prague, Czech Republic

There is a section of Prague, Czech Republic called Wenceslas Square. The National Museum is there and has the type of columns, windows, spires, and steeples that I enjoy drawing. Near the front of the Museum is a wonderful statue called the Wenceslas Monument, so I leaned my drawing pad on the statue's pedestal and proceeded to sketch, looking up at the statue and across at the building.

I find this type of architecture especially enjoyable to sketch, since the combination of window shapes and window placement always has fascinated me. I think about why the architect would use this particular placement pattern of shapes, and realize that the positioning of these architectural elements is what gives this building its stately look.

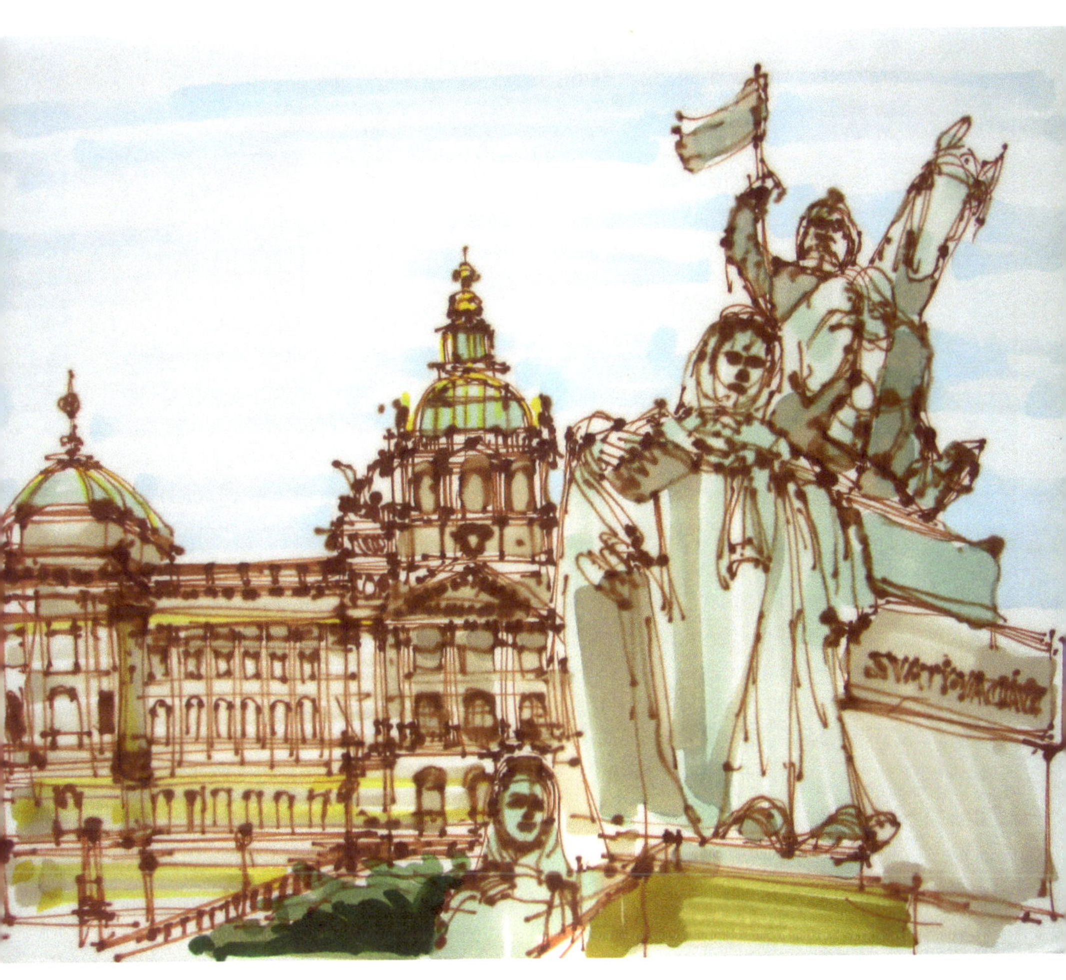
SVATOVACLAVSKÉ

The Big Foreground Statue

Again, the large foreground object is an important part of this sketch. The foreground object adds dimension to the sketch, leading the viewer's eye into key architectural elements.

For the statue in the foreground, first outline its position on your paper so that you know the object will fit comfortably with the rest of your sketch.

Ponte Vecchio, Florence

Along the Arno River in Florence, Italy is a series of picturesque bridges, the most famous of which is the Ponte Vecchio. I wanted to sketch this famous bridge among the many bridges that spanned the river, so I walked over and stood on the Ponte Santa Trinita Bridge to capture the view of the Ponte Vecchio structures and its arches. One of the "Four Seasons" statues was just in front of where I was standing, and I used it to add dimension to the drawing. When you have the opportunity to use an interesting foreground object – for example an illustrious statue – it also adds relevance to your drawing.

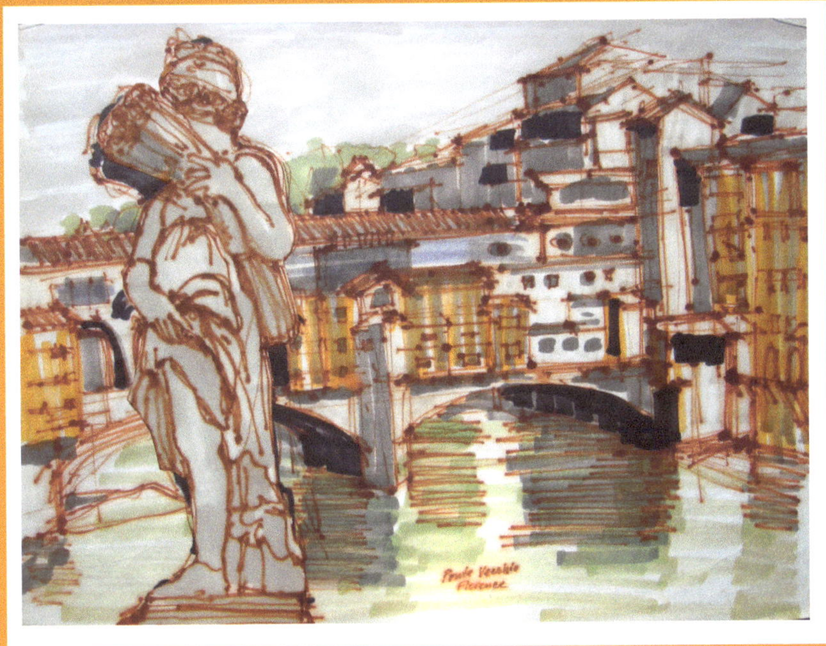

Ponte Vecchio
Florence

Tai-O, Hong Kong

This drawing was made in a Hong Kong area called Tai-O that had a special fascination to me. It consisted of homes and stores that were built on bamboo, and life within these bamboo structures was like a little town unto itself. The overall effect was an architectural element that I had never seen before – with ladders, platforms, cubicles, and housing.

By making this drawing, I have a strong memory of the way that the bamboo sticks pulled together to create the structure. I will always remember the feeling that I had when recognizing that people working within the structure inhabit and raise their children there. Boats moved in and out. Although many parts of the world have small fishing houses along the shoreline, I believe there are none as unique as the structures made by these bamboo poles.

The two boats in the foreground of this sketch lead the viewer's eye into the water and give a third dimension to the two-dimensional view of the unique bamboo structure. Boats serve well as foreground objects in a drawing -- keep in mind that the boats shift around in the water, so sketch the position you prefer as soon as possible during your drawing time.

I made this drawing from the shore on the opposite part of the inlet, and while sketching I felt that I was in a location where very few people have been. I saw no one near me while I was sketching. And yet there was much going on within the bamboo structure across the inlet, and the entire scene to me not only was fascinating but made for one of my favorite days of travel.

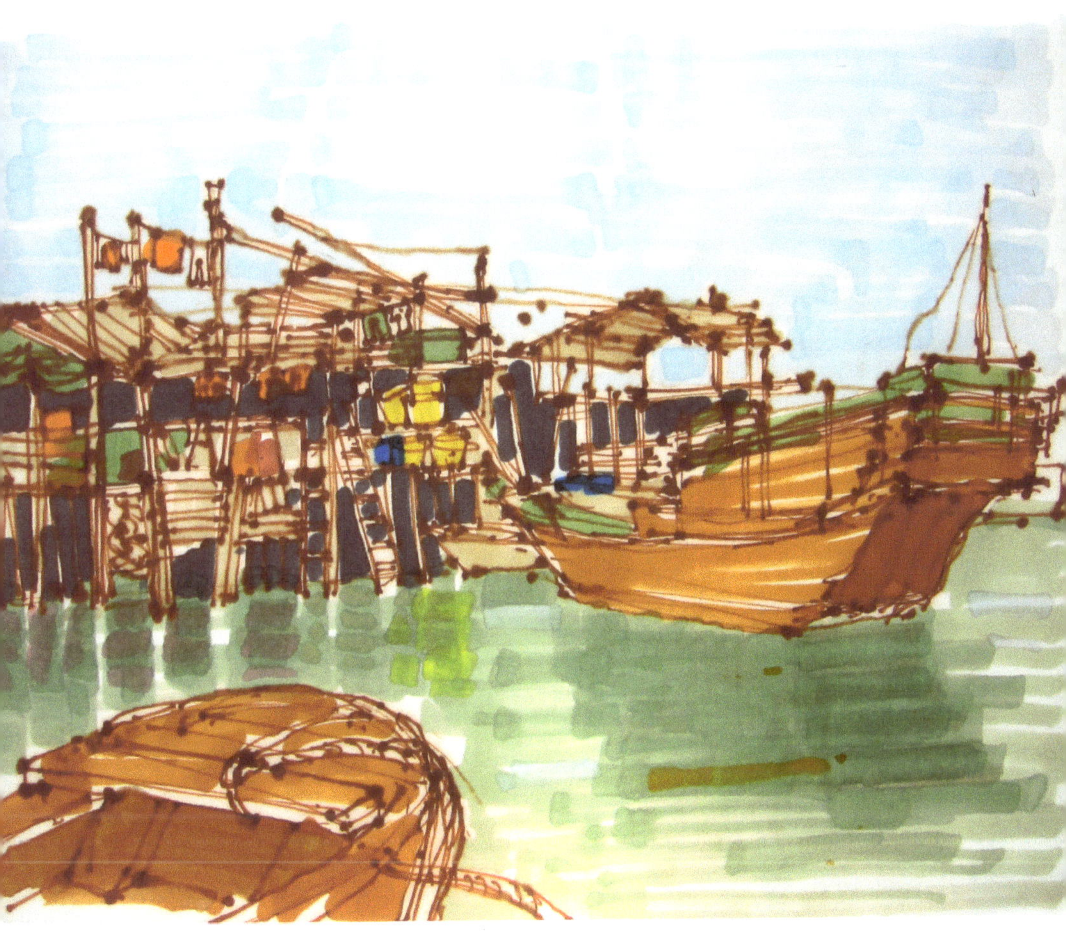

Sketching People

During your travels, drawing people can be challenging for many reasons. We are all familiar with the proportions of human beings, and an inexperienced artist often has difficulty drawing people with reasonable proportions. There are ways to overcome this. Keep in mind that adding a human helps define the scale of your drawing and makes a drawing of a scene or structure become animate. But we need to sketch quickly, since people move around!

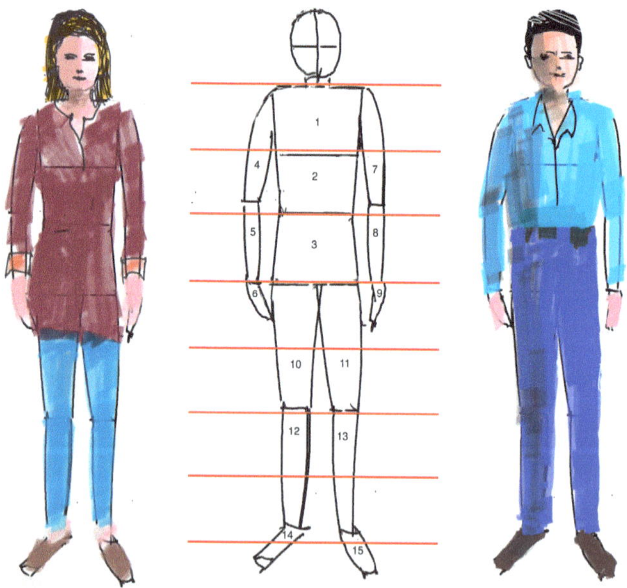

Proportionately, adults are 7 to 8 heads tall, as shown above. For sketching, you can think of the human body having 15 spatial areas plus the head. In simple terms, this includes (1) upper torso, (2) mid torso, (3) lower torso, (4) upper arm, (5) lower arm, (6) hand, (7) upper arm, (8) lower arm, (9) hand, (10) upper leg, (11) upper leg, (12) lower leg, (13) lower leg, (14) foot, (15) foot. Practice drawing a friend or relative by sketching in these 15 areas before applying skin and clothing colors, and you may get your best results. On the following pages, note how these 15 areas are sketched prior to the addition of color.

Practice sketching people quickly. During your travels, the people you sketch will likely be moving from place to place, so it's helpful to use a quick sketching method.

Think of those 15 spatial areas of the human body and try to capture them. When you are satisfied with the line work, add your color and shading. Keep your drawing loose, without much detail, and you will have time to move on to your next subject.

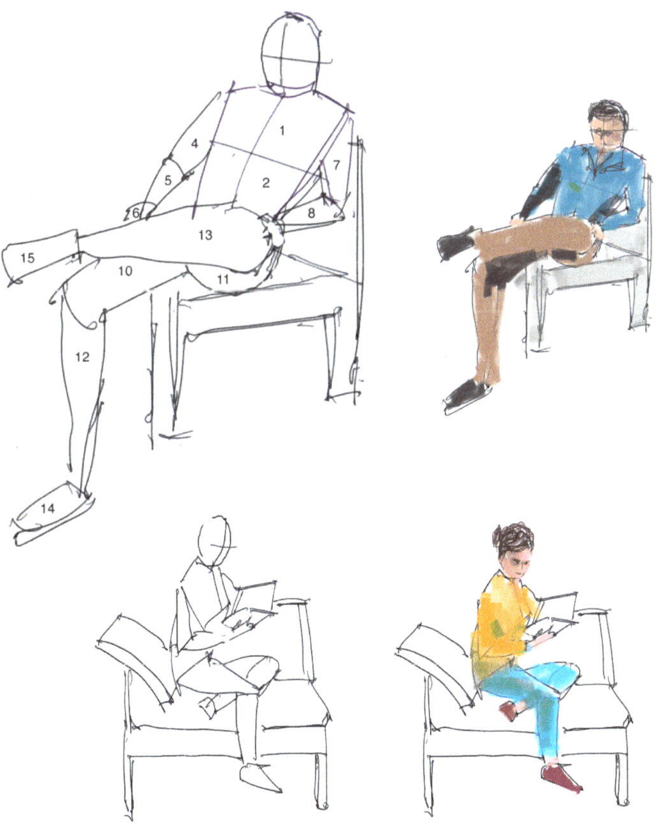

Western Wall, Jerusalem

The Western Wall In Jerusalem is probably the most sacred site for the Jewish people. Known as the "Wailing Wall" it was built over 2000 years ago. Tourists come from all over the world to see the Wall and Jews from the more religious to the moderately religious will go there and pray against the Wall itself. People go during daytime and nighttime to pray and observe there, and special services like bar mitzvahs are also held at the Wall.

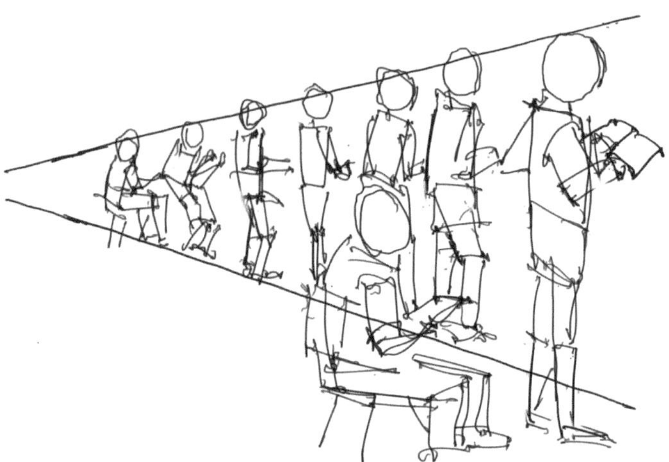

With luck you may find a single person or a group of people to sketch that are sitting or standing still. This line sketch above was made of men praying — standing still — at the Western Wall in Jerusalem during my travels there. By sketching quickly I was able to capture the men praying before they shifted, and the result with the color application is shown on the next page...

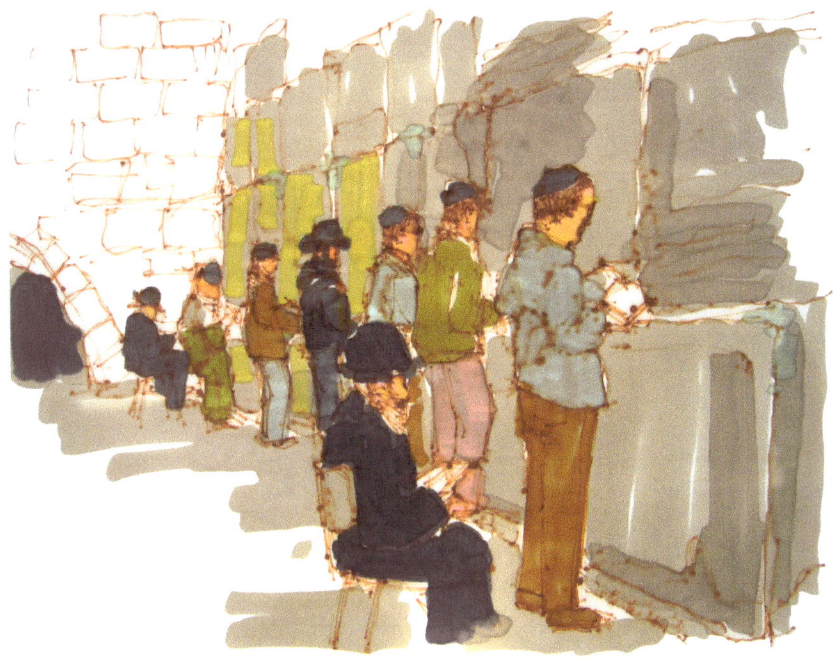

This is a drawing that is rarely made. There may be photographs of people at the Wall but I have never before heard of anybody making a drawing at the scene. I felt that it was a very touching scene and I wanted to record it as I saw it creatively -- of very serious men standing against the Wall in 'their own world,' thinking carefully about what they are saying and not really paying attention to the people around them. I leaned my drawing pad on the back of a chair to make the sketch.

The men stand against the Wall with prayer books and pray and some leave notes in the Wall as notes of remembrance. It was a stirring scene, and I also felt that the muted colors added to the scene. There are religious men in the drawing as well as men in a more secular fashion mode. The color of the stones and the muted color of the clothing makes for an interesting drawing.

Fruit Truck, Jaipur, India

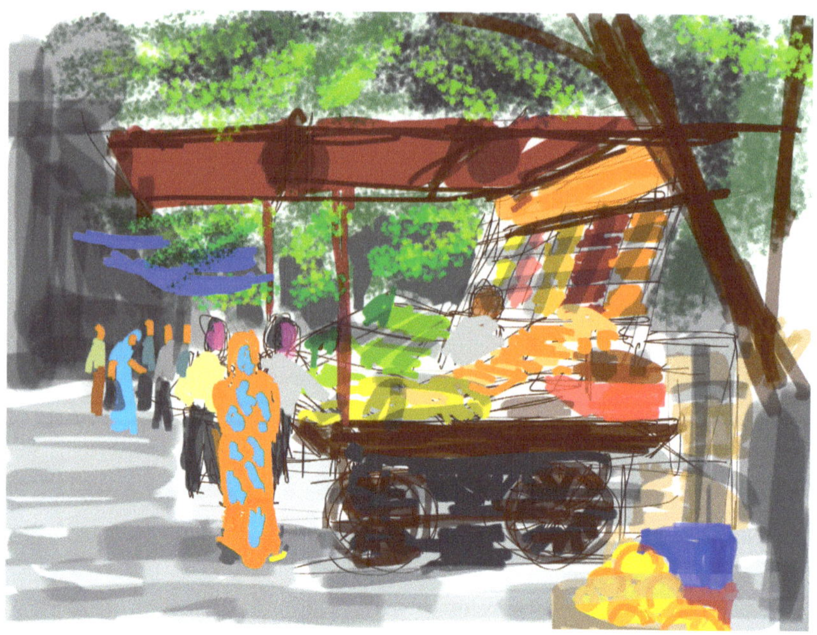

While walking around a fruit market in Jaipur, India I spotted this particular cart, which I thought made a colorful scene with its canopy, products, and shoppers.

Note the importace of the people in the scene. Their clothing and the sari on the woman in the foreground helped the drawing's composition and depth.

Although I kept it sketchy, the overall effect was colorful. Once again, there was no place actually to put my iPad while drawing, so I just stood and held the iPad in my hand while I was drawing. I had to sketch quickly. When finished, I showed the drawing to the food cart owner, which he enjoyed and also requested that I give him a tip, so I did give him a small amount of money out of gratitude.

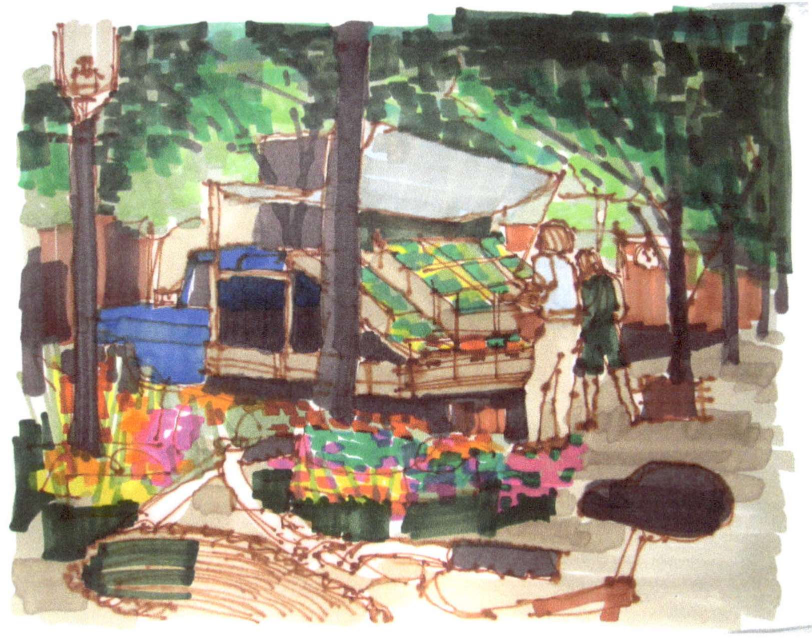

Without people in this sketch. it would be difficult to understand the elements of the scene -- how the vegetable truck is utilized and its placement on the street. The people add comprehension and scale to the drawing.

Every day on Nantucket's Main Street there is a truck parked with flowers and vegetables from which residents and passersby purchase products. It is a charming and colorful scene in small-town America. By drawing the truck with its surroundings, I was able to really concentrate on the set-up that has been there daily for many years -- the presentation of the products as well as the canopy above the truck, making an interesting scene to draw.

The flowers add bright color. For depth, I included a bicycle that was parked in the foreground, since you will usually find bicycles on the sidewalk there.

Elephanta Island near Mumbai, India

The scene is overwhelming when one arrives in Mumbai, India, with what we would consider chaotic streets filled with people, cars, taxis, cows, goats and every market variety of food. The neighborhoods in the large city of Mumbai change drastically, displaying wealth along with poverty, and the tours of the temples, museums and local streets are fascinating.

From Mumbai we boarded a small boat that held about 30 people and traveled for one hour to Elephanta Island. From the boat we embarked to a train for about one and a half miles and then to the stone steps that lead us up to the caves on Elephanta Island. It's a long climb up the steps, which are spread apart from one another, and since it is over a mountain, some of the steps are on a much steeper pitch than others. Since there are about 120 of those steps, I figured this is my opportunity for a little exercise, even though I was carrying a fairly heavy bag with my art equipment.

Once we got to the top, it was a sight to behold -- caves that were built out of the rock in the mountain in the seventh century. Great sculptures of Indian gods in various activities of life, death and marriage were carved out of the mountain rock. The sculptures in the caves are dedicated to the trinity of the Indian deities, which are Brahma, Vishnu and Shiva. The cave architecture was quite exciting, with many huge columns carved from the stone which give a monumental feeling throughout.

The person standing in this sketch emphasizes the enormity of the columns that were carved 1300 years ago. I politely informed our tour guide that I would like to do some drawing and found a seat on high stone steps that faced the columns.

As soon as I started to bring out my sketchpad and art equipment, people in the area were quite interested in seeing what I had in mind, and several dozen who were touring the area came over to watch what I was doing. It made me a bit self-conscious, but I set up the sketchpad and started sketching. I was intrigued by the elements of the architecture, the cutting and size of the stone, the amount of columns that the builders chose to use, the rounded forms on the square forms, and how all the units in the architecture connected to one another. It's amazing that the carving, planning and ideas at that time led to the way today's builders use columns in their construction and decoration.

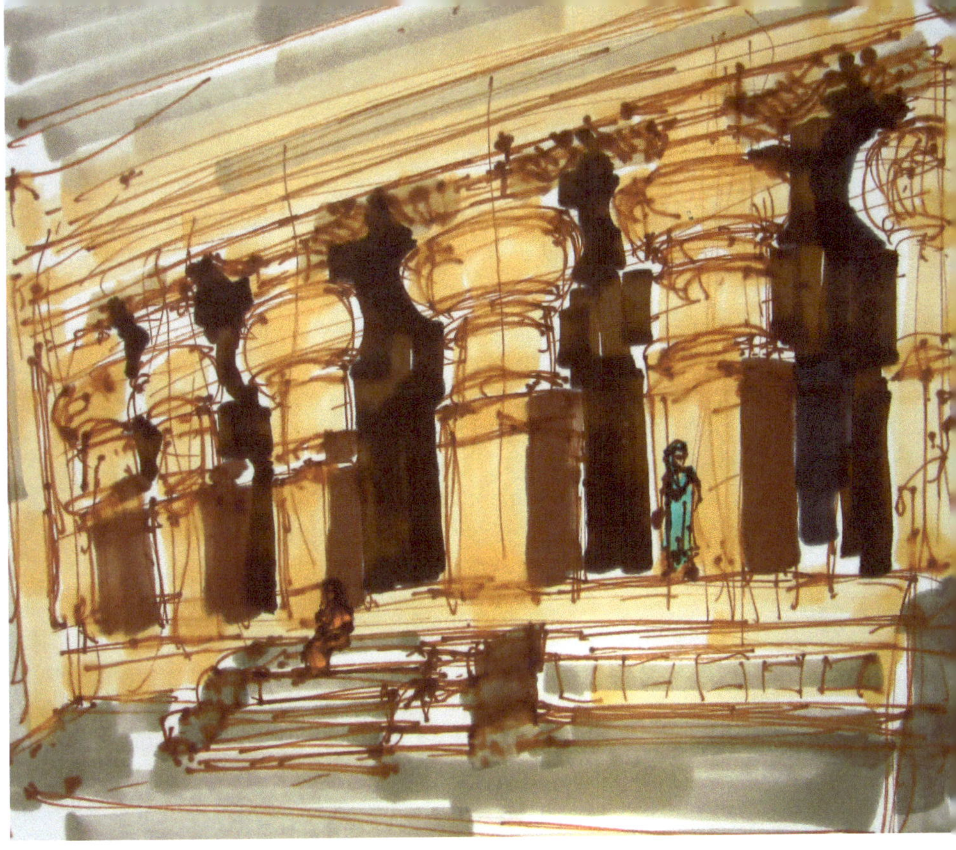

The sketch took perhaps 45 minutes. During that time, I thought about what
the builders were thinking and why they placed the columns the distance from
one another. Why did the builders decide to cut the stone to that particular
height? This we will never know. But in their minds, I presume it gave a
monumental appearance and they felt it was the right thing to do. So as I
sketched, I concentrated on each of these factors and on the coloration of the
stone -- yellowish in some areas, gray in some areas, and in some areas a
combination of both.

In some parts of the world people are more intrigued by watching someone
sketch than in others. Here, the Indian people were interested in watching the
development of the sketch. There were even people there from a local news-
paper who stopped to take pictures of me and ask a few questions about why
I preferred sketching to photography.

An Huu, Vietnam

This drawing was made in a small town named An Huu, near Danang. As we were driving toward Danang, I noticed a village that looked intriguing with rural Vietnamese character. We spent some time on the Danang River with a boat tour and later, when driving back, came upon this village once again. The driver stopped for me and we walked from a sparse area to the banks of this river inlet that was part of An Huu.

I set up my sketchpad on a table and found a chair and proceeded to sketch the dock, the 2 people, and a background of buildings that were rather color-ful and gave a feeling of river life and character. The bridge on which we had driven to get to where I was drawing connected these buildings to my side of the shore.

As I was making this drawing, things were constantly changing. The light changed in the two hours or so it took to make the drawing. Boats on the water moved in different directions and people moved around as well. But I was able to catch most of the elements and gave depth to the sketch by emphasizing the men's bright shirt colors and the dock in the foreground.. This enabled the water and the buildings in the background to visually recede, so that the overall picture is one of depth and color to reflect that part of Vietnam.

In Vietnam, people were very interested in watching me draw and this was certainly no exception. Many ages from very young to very old came out at different periods to watch me and there were probably a total of 30 to 40 people from the neighborhood that stopped by to see what I was doing. I was happy to talk with anyone willing to speak English, but spent most of the time concentrating on the drawing.

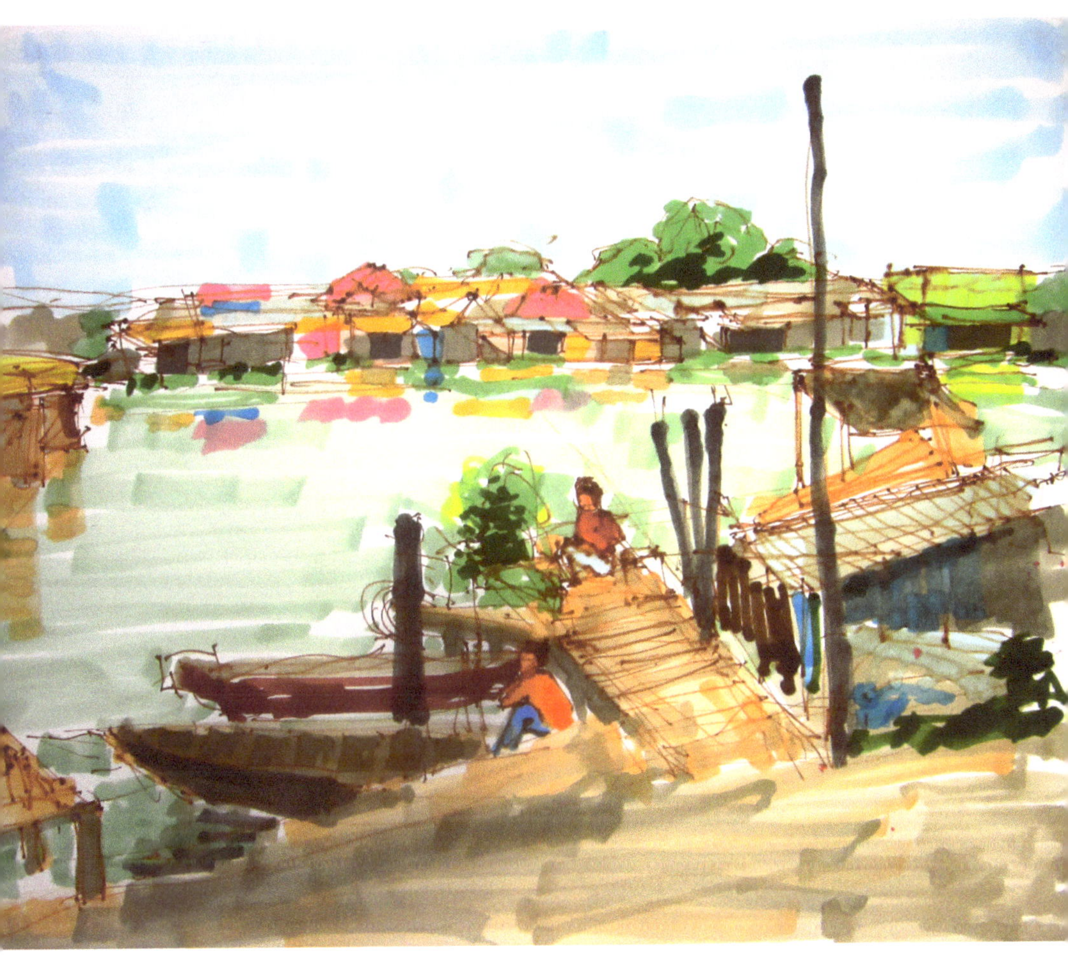

Sketching close-ups or portraits require a different kind of attention to details. The face shape, eyes, nose, mouth, chin, and neck now become a noticeable part of your drawing. While traveling, you'll rarely have much time to concentrate on every detail. And if you don't know the person you are sketching, it's more important to capture the fundamentals than the resemblance.

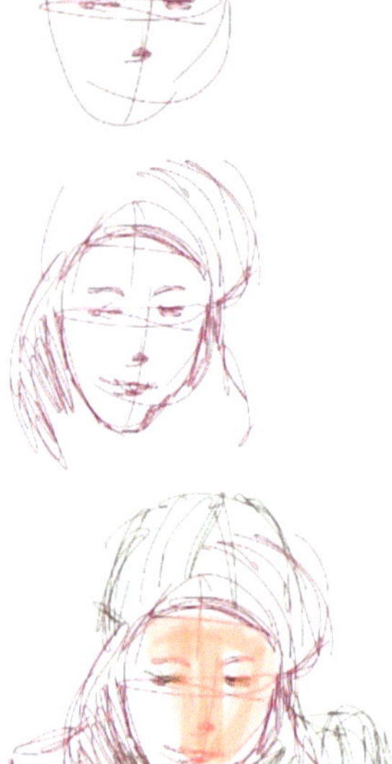

The following steps will enable you to draw a close-up without spending too much time.

Start with an oval shape for the face with a vertical line down the center of the oval and a horizontal line across the center of the oval. Locate the two eyes and the bottom of the nose.

Add the cheeks, chin, mouth, hair (or hat) and the shapes of the eyes and eyebrows.

Add surrounding elements to include the neck, shoulders and proportional upper body. Add clothing detail and start adding skin color.

Finalize your drawing with darker skin color for shading, eye color, lip color, hair color and clothing colors. Do not overwork your drawing – keep it sketchy and it will blend well with your other travel drawings.

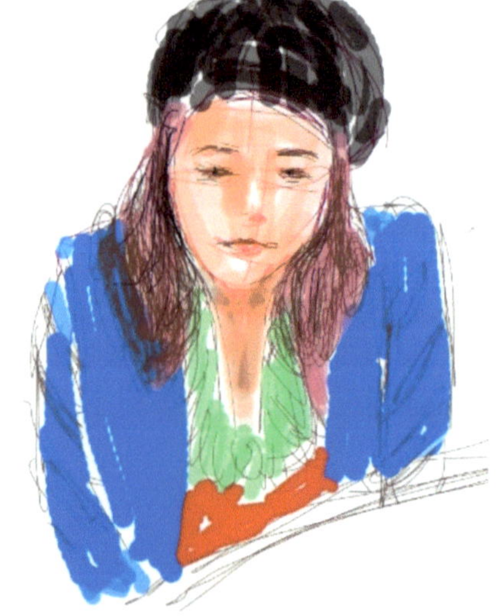

Forgive me if I make it look too easy. However, with practice you will definitely keep improving while enjoying the experience!

Sketching Trees

Trees and bushes become elements to make any structure look friendly, the way the trees and bushes help your home do the same. I see them as functionally decorative elements on any drawing and they should also be handled in an efficient and sketchy manner. Most often, standard colors will work for the trees and bushes in your drawing, and I recommend using Grass Green, Yellow Green, Dark Green, Olive and Medium Gray.

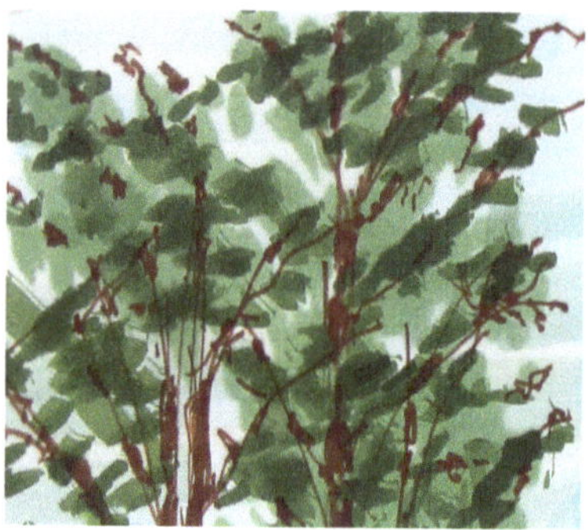 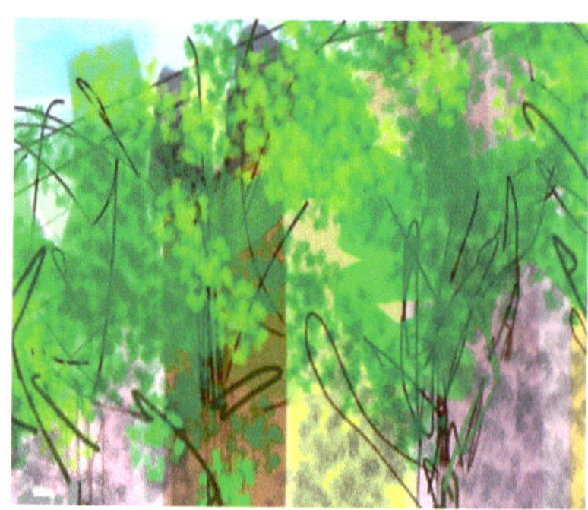

I first put in the Grass Green color, leaving white spaces for light or any other color that might become part of the tree or the bush. Based on the outdoor conditions, you then add one layer of Dark Green shading, leaving the Grass Green color in the areas that receive more light. You then add a layer of Olive or Gray shading to define the shape of the tree or bush and to create shadows where appropriate.

Once your trees and bushes have been defined and colored as they appear to your eye, you use the fine tip Brown or Gray marker to add tree trunks or tree branches to the trees, with the brown lines disappearing and reappearing under the leafy areas. If there are brightly, sunlit leaves on the trees, you can add Yellow Green to those areas as your tree structure takes shape.

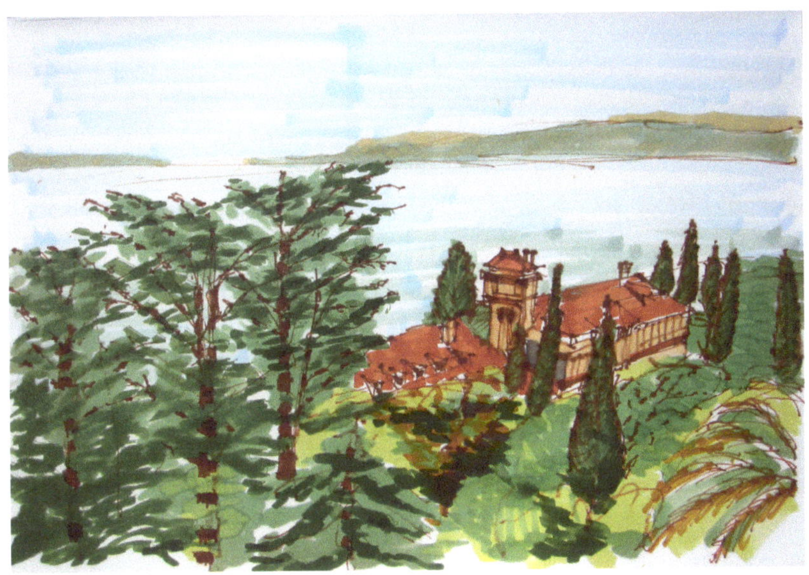

Lake Garda, in the northern part of Italy, is the largest of Italy's freshwater lakes. There are many charming towns around the circumference of the lake and the traveler can go from town to town via ferryboat that leaves quite often from different ports on the lake. With its wonderful views from each of these towns, Lake Garda is a popular holiday vacation area with interesting places for sketching. Each town around the lake has its own special characteristics and charm and I would highly recommend it as a place for sketching and enjoying the sights and capturing the beauty of the lake and its towns.

For someone who enjoys drawing scenery and architecture, try to find a place to stay -- a hotel or a house -- that overlooks a good view. On Lake Garda, the Hotel Villa Sostaga where I stayed was on a hill and looked down the hillside into the lake. I viewed this red roof structure and trees that became a good subject for my drawing. The combination of the tall trees plus the cypress trees and red roof building gave my drawing its focus and a spot of color.

Bellano, Italy

When driving along the many curvy roads around Lake Como, Italy, I passed an overlook that completely charmed me. I stopped the car and parked in an area close to the spot from where I could view this scene showing trees, mountains, railroad tracks, water and small boats. I was overwhelmed by the way the houses were built on the mountain, as though they were on top of each other, and just below these houses was a railroad track that was extremely close to the water's edge. In the water were small boats, which added to this charming scene. In the background I could see some rolling hills and I felt it was important to capture a view such as this, that one only sees a few times in a lifetime. To me, the view was extraordinary and I found a place to stand and lean my drawing pad in order to capture the charm of the scene.

Note: the leaves and branches in the left foreground add depth to the drawing.

It started drizzling while I was sketching so it was rather uncomfortable trying to keep the sketchpad as dry as possible while working on the drawing. The rain became a little stronger, the pad started getting wet, but I felt that I had to finish this drawing and kept working on it until it was complete. It is not often that you view scenery in any part of the world that gives the charm of this small town of Bellano, Italy on Lake Como.

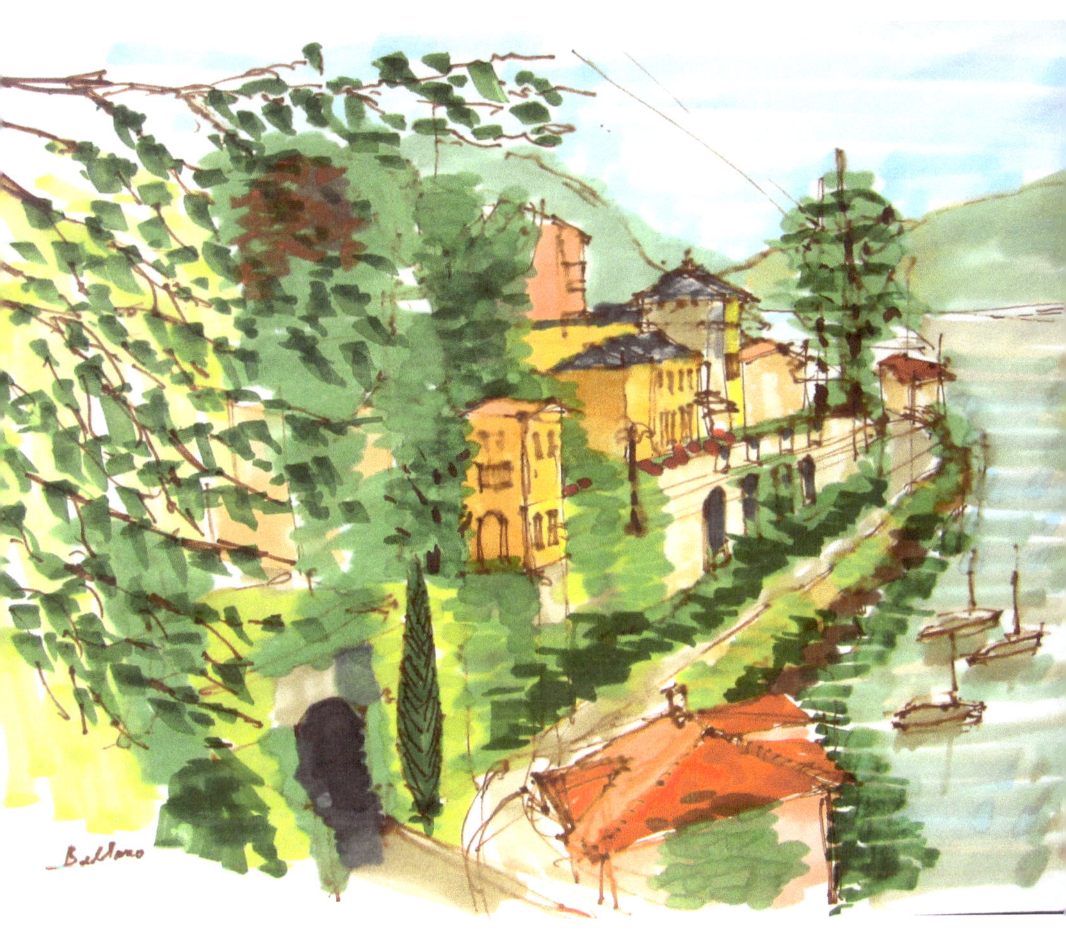

Bellano

Brouwersgract Canal, Amsterdam

The picturesque canals running through Amsterdam make it a wonderful city in which to sketch. The reflections of the boats and buildings on the canals are colorful and the bright hues of the buildings themselves make their own statement.

Before applying the trees to this iPad sketch, I drew all the basic elements. This gave me the perspective and structure of the drawing, as you see below. I then sketched in the trees --- first the outlines, next the Dark Green, and then the Lighter Greens to emphasize the leaves. I dabbled Light Grey to show the shadows cast from the trees on the buildings. Compare the sketch below to the finished iPad sketch on the opposite page. The water reflects tree colors and building colors.

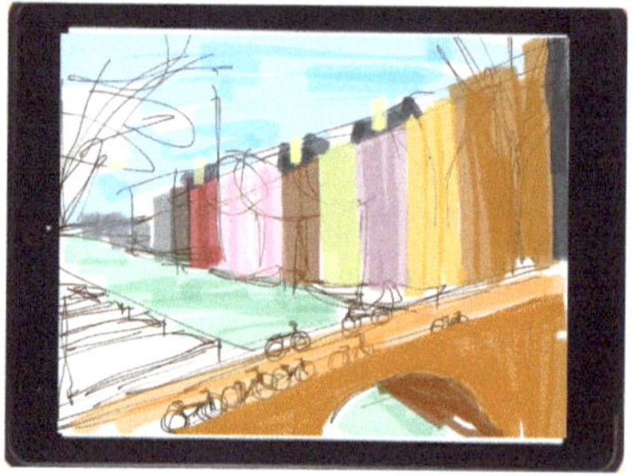

The bridge across the Brouwersgract Canal combines buildings and trees that form an interesting composition.. I felt that the bicycles parked on the sides of the bridge walkway suggested the flavor of Amsterdam, since Amsterdam is really a city full of bicycles. I did not want to leave Amsterdam without including bicycles in at least one of my iPad sketches.

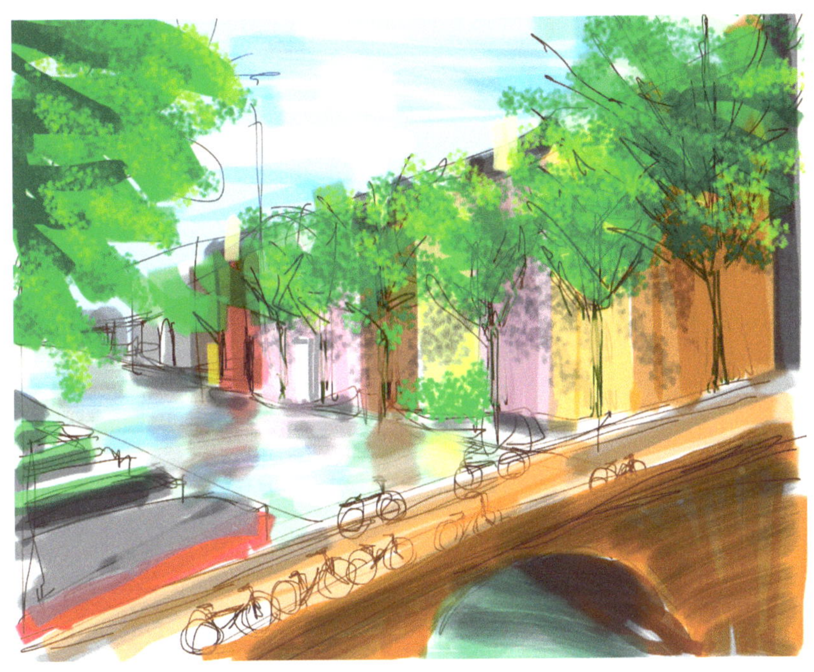

Stratton Mountain, Vermont

This sketch of Vermont trees in autumn has a more impressionist style than most of the other drawings in the book. For the elements in the scene, I used the full, broad strokes of the color markers so that I could emphasize the colors rather than the precise shapes of the trees or the leaves. The overall effect of the drawing is colorful and a bit abstract, and I appreciate the results portrayed by these bright, autumn colors.

The water and reflections from the trees are critical to this sketch, and you may refer to the guide for "Sketching Water and Reflections" in that chapter of this book.

Stratton Mountain, where this skech was made, is part of the Green Mountain Range in Vermont. It's in the southern part of Vermont and is one of the resort areas attractive to many skiers in the winter and also in summer, since the resort includes golf, hiking, mountain biking and swimming. Although most of the time that I've spent at Stratton has been in the winter for skiing, I also enjoy the change of the leaves in fall. Normally the brightest colors are during the second and third week of October and it's a treat to drive around southern Vermont to see the leaves in their glory.

On one of the trips there during the fall I couldn't resist walking over to this pond and seeing the pines together with the oak and birch and many other species of trees with their bright, fall leaves.

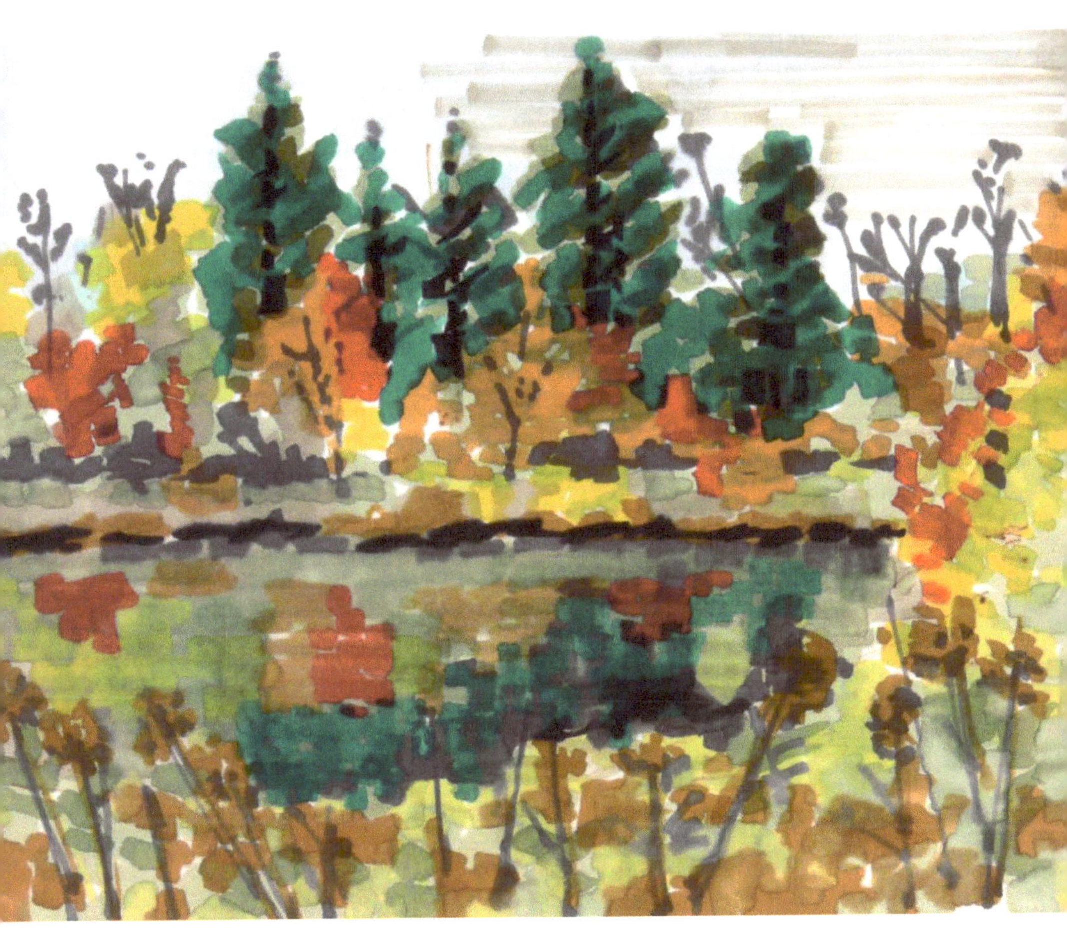

Sketching Trees on the iPad

This iPad drawing, made in my backyard during a colorful autumn season, addressed an efficient method for rendering trees, leaves, and their coloration.

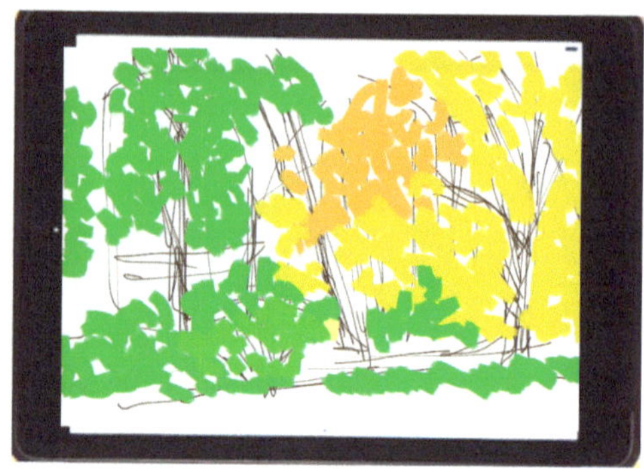

As always, I start by framing the scene with a thin dark line and minimum color to balance and contain the elements for the selected area. The first colors applied are Leaf green, Light green, Medium Yellow, and Light Orange.

After filling the area with these basic colors, I then apply Dark Green, Olive, Light Brown, and Umber to represent the brighter areas and the shaded areas.

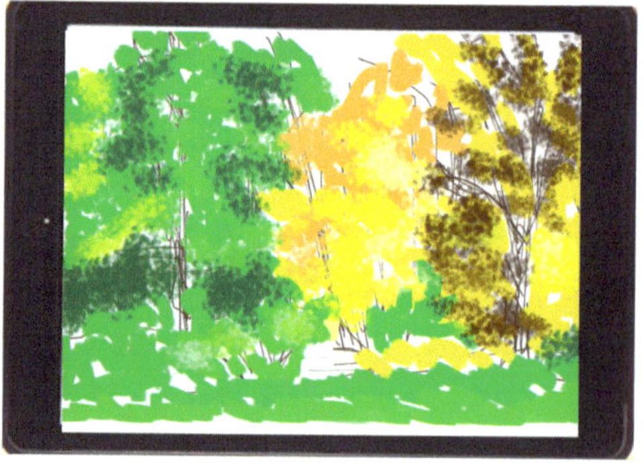

I then introduce the tree structures, using Umber color for all of the trees and the branches. You will note that the branches break up within the leaves, which gives the impression of leaves growing on and covering up some of those branches, as typical for all trees.

Final touches are added, including Light Blue in the sky and additional dabs of Yellow and Brown near the ground. The result is a spontaneous rendering of the colorful part of the season.

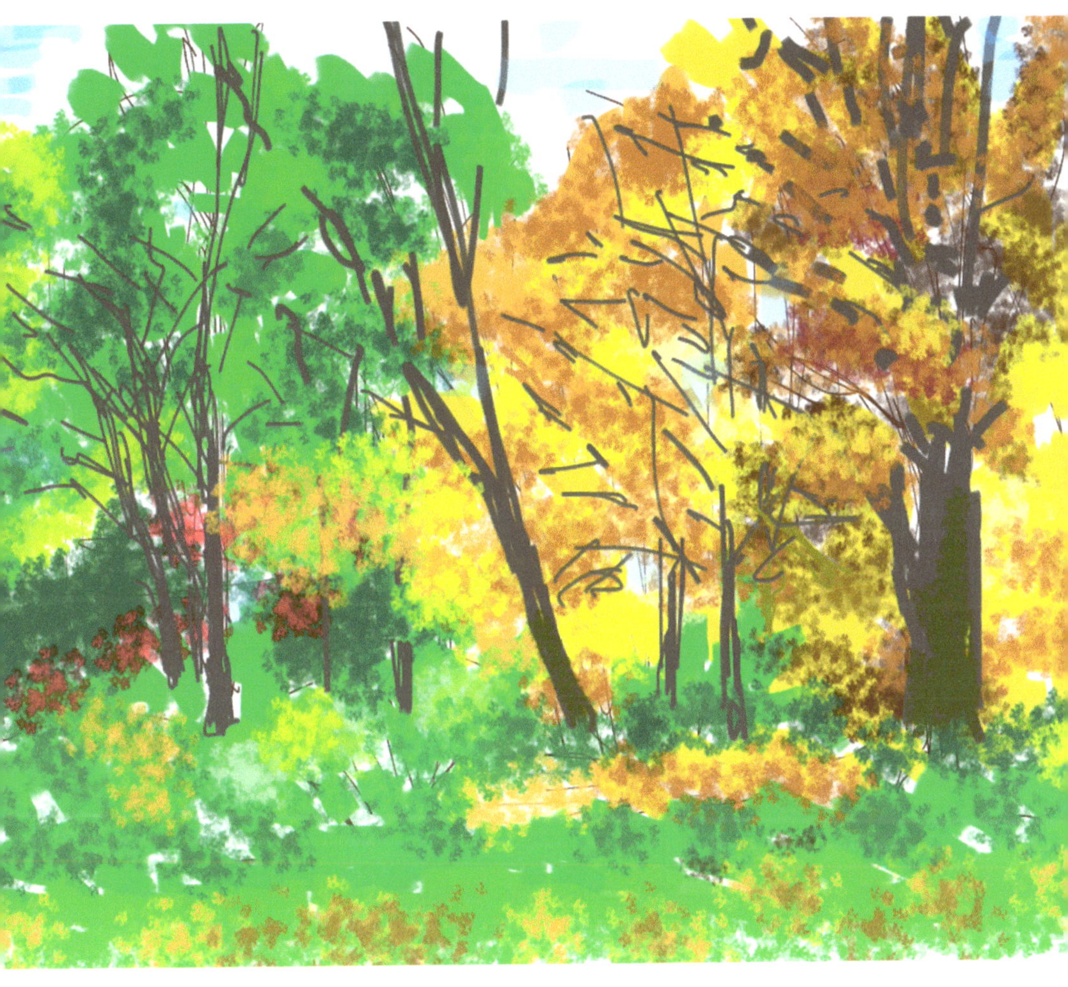

Windows and Steeples

To me, the most interesting thing about the windows that I see when I travel is the question of how they apply to the architecture. When someone takes a photo of a famous landmark building, they rarely if ever consider what the architect had in mind for the windows. When sketching a building, you become fully aware of the window's size, quantity, configuration, and placement. You may ask yourself, "Why did the architect put three windows on this roof rather than two windows?" For every one of these landmark structures, there was a reason for the placement of the windows and the shape of the windows. By sketching them you have to look closely at them, think about them, and remember forever their architectural narrative.

So take advantage of the opportunity to observe and study the windows. Sketch them quickly, but indicate their shapes, so that they help to enhance the structure that you are sketching.

On the opposite page you will note in my drawing that the shapes of the windows are drawn in a sketchy manner to save time, but yet those shapes are indicated and proportioned, and their quantity is implied. Archways and steeples also hold architectural interest, often with dramatic shapes and proportions to define the landmark building.

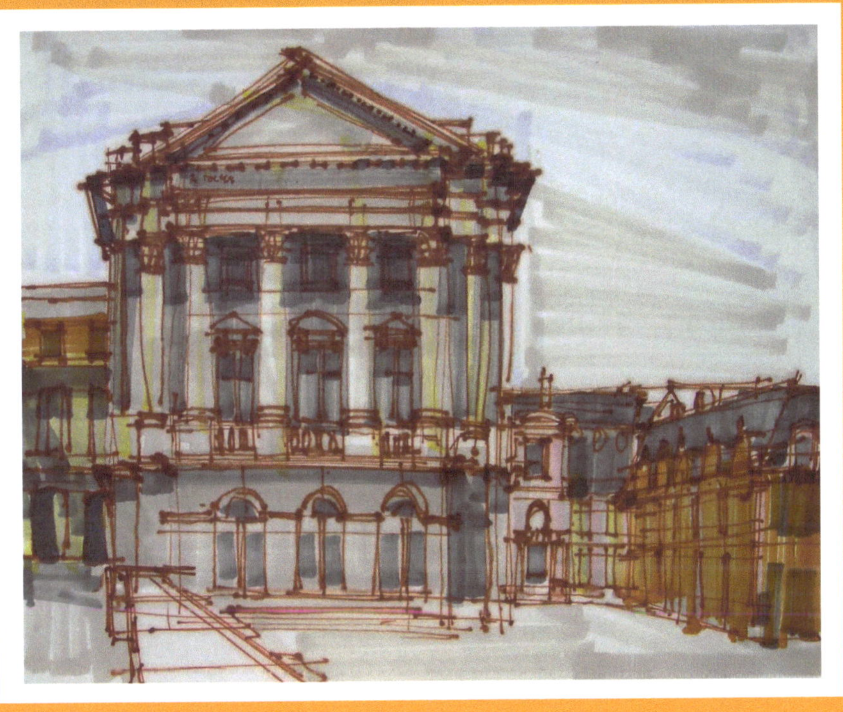

Steeples in Budapest, Hungary

When traveling throughout the world, some of the most interesting buildings that I have enjoyed sketching have unique types of steeples – sometimes they are religious buildings and sometimes they are government buildings. For thousands of years the architects and builders have used the steeples as a method of expressing their own creativity, identity, and cultural attitude.

When sketching the steeples, take the time to reflect their shape and proportion relating to the rest of the structure. Although they can be rendered in a sketchy manner, I have learned how interesting and unique each steeple is from the other in different parts of the world.

The steeples are enjoyable to draw because of their shape and symmetry. You should also try to capture the horizontal and vertical elements of the steeples that add interest to the drawing.

There are many interesting landmarks all around Budapest, Hungary. However, without much time to sketch there, I tried to pick spots that were unusually picturesque, and this scene on the following page, a walking distance from my hotel, fascinated me because it seemed like a structure right out of the 15th century. While making this drawing, I was able to study the shape of the roofs, the steeples, and the shape of the architectural elements in such a way that one could never understand it through a photograph.

I made a series of sketches of the buildings in this area, since they all had fascinating architectural elements. Some of them contained unique domes and roofs that were memorable and would not have been closely observed if I was just taking a photograph.

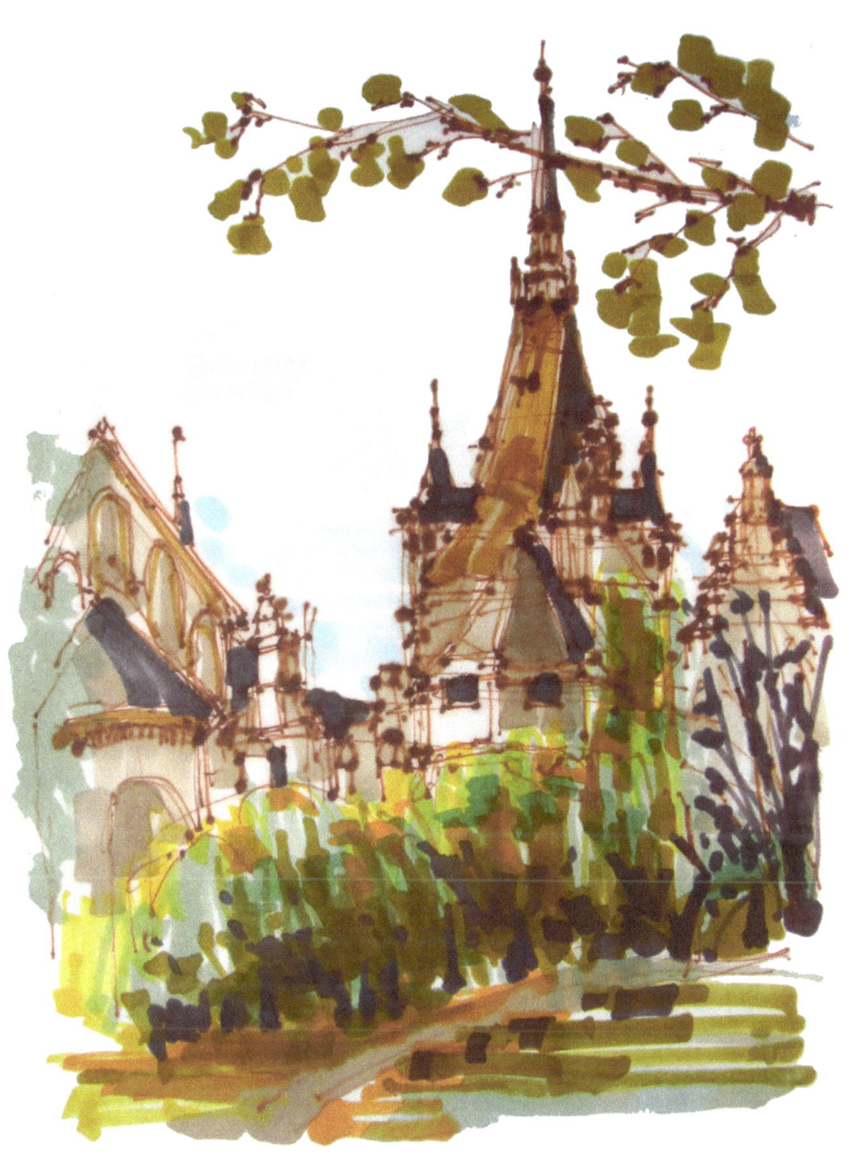

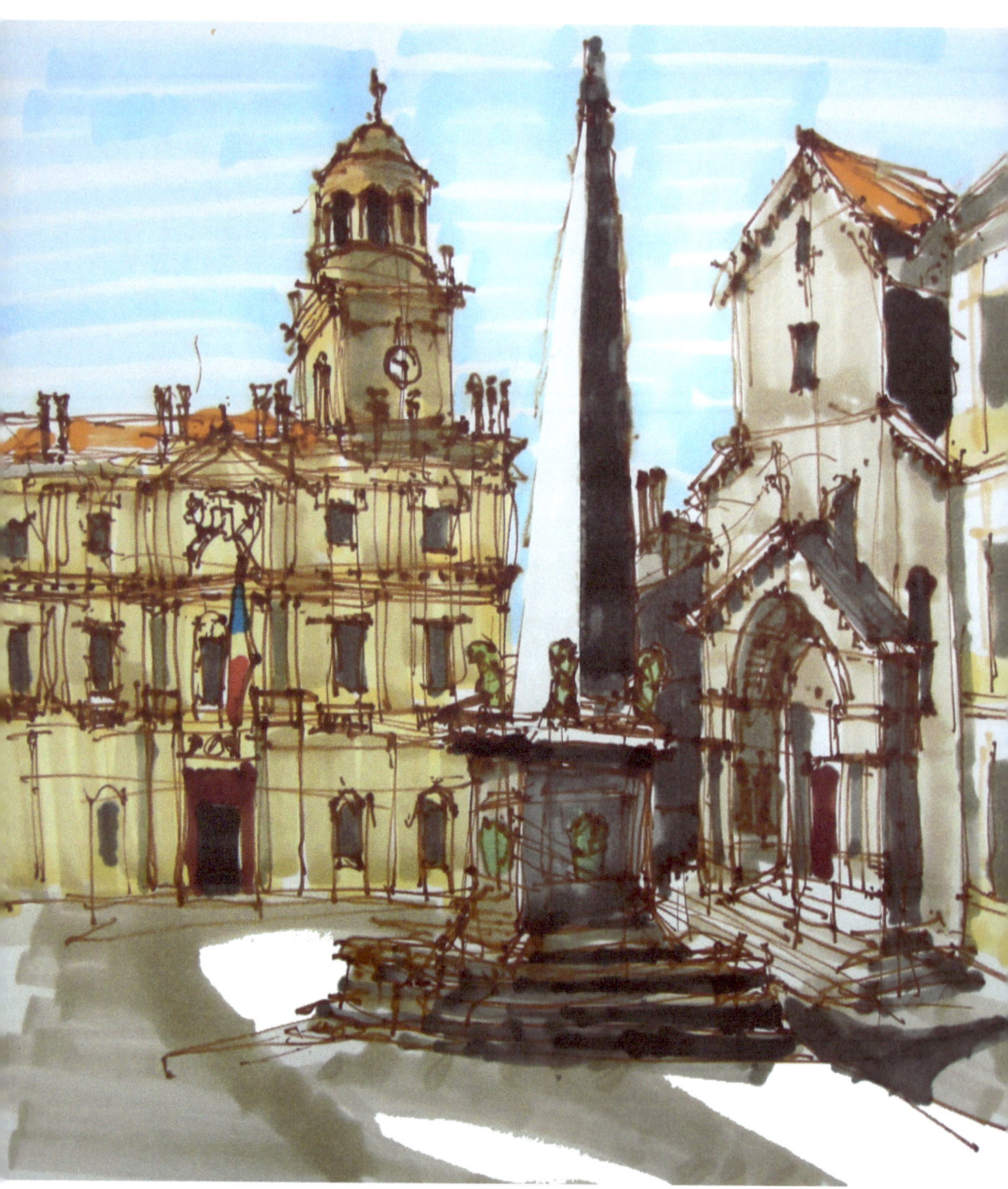

Plaza de la Republique, Arles, France

Arles is the town that is famous for Vincent van Gogh. Through the years I had read about Arles and the scenes that van Gogh painted there, so to me this city always had a very romantic image. I was determined to travel to Arles, a city that covers a large area and is encircled by exceptional beauty. It is on the banks of the Rhône River and the river delta land of Comargue.

Arriving in Arles, it appeared to be a larger town than I had expected, and much of it -- including many parts of its waterfront -- had been modernized. The town was a maze of alleyways and streets working their way to the Rhône River. I was looking for a place to sketch along the waterfront and started walking along the adjacent roads. In Arles the river is wide with high walls and there was little that inspired me to sketch there, especially since there were no interesting boats along the Rhône at the time. The bridges had been rebuilt and had a modern look, and the views revealed mainly newer buildings, rather than the older buildings that lurked in the alleyways and streets further inland.

I walked for about 3 miles looking for sketching sites and then came upon the Plaza de la Republique, where several weddings were taking place. This was a charming area, which included the central theme cloister, a Romanesque church, and the City Hall (Hotel DeVille). When I first had arrived there, the plaza was filled with hundreds of people who had attended the weddings in the Plaza. By the time I finished setting up for sketching, many people had dispersed and I ended up having the Plaza somewhat to myself. There was no spot to actually place my drawing pad except on the easel that I was carrying, so I used my easel and spent about two hours making the drawing of the Plaza de la Republique and its structures.

Windows, steeples, and arches are all part of these Romanesque structures, and if an artist wants to spend much time and show the details, it would be an interesting project. However in order to move from site to site, and finish the sketches within an appropriate amount of time for traveling, you may do as I did -- show the window locations without drawing the details.

Notre Dame de Paris

Notre Dame is probably the world's most famous Gothic cathedral. Located in the Ile de Cite in Paris it is easily recognizable to everybody passing through. It was among the first buildings in the world to use the flying buttress as part of its architecture.

When arriving there, my challenge was to find a suitable location from which to sketch and set up my drawing pad and markers and materials that are part of the drawing process. I walked around the cathedral and found a street perpendicular to the cathedral on the opposite side of the Seine River. I sat down on a step near the sidewalk, placed my pad on a low wall and proceeded to draw. Interestingly, there was a gentleman about 40 feet in front of me who was also drawing the cathedral. However, I could see that he had been there for a long time with his drawing, since he was using pencil and was deliniating every imaginable detail of the cathedral, a process that would probably take him several weeks to complete. I noticed that he was working on the rose window and doing a portion of it while I was drawing the same overall cathedral structure.

I framed out my drawing and concentrated on making the lines look quick and confident so that it would convey the theme of the buttresses of the cathedral itself. I felt it was not important for me to deal with the minute details, since the overall structure made such a fine architectural statement.

I really felt that, in the 1 1/2 hours that I made my drawing, I was able to understand the church architecture – its rose window, it's flying buttresses, the many Gothic arches and steeples and shapes that were part of the cathedral. When drawing you can see the individually crafted statues around the outside serving as column supports and waterspouts. Among these are the unique gargoyles, which were designed for water runoff. Although my mission was not to draw every detail, I still felt that I had learned a lot about Notre Dame's architecture, from the spacing of the windows, to the centering of the rose window, to the placing of the cross, and even the shrubberies that surrounded it. I was satisfied that I had achieved the spirit of the cathedral.

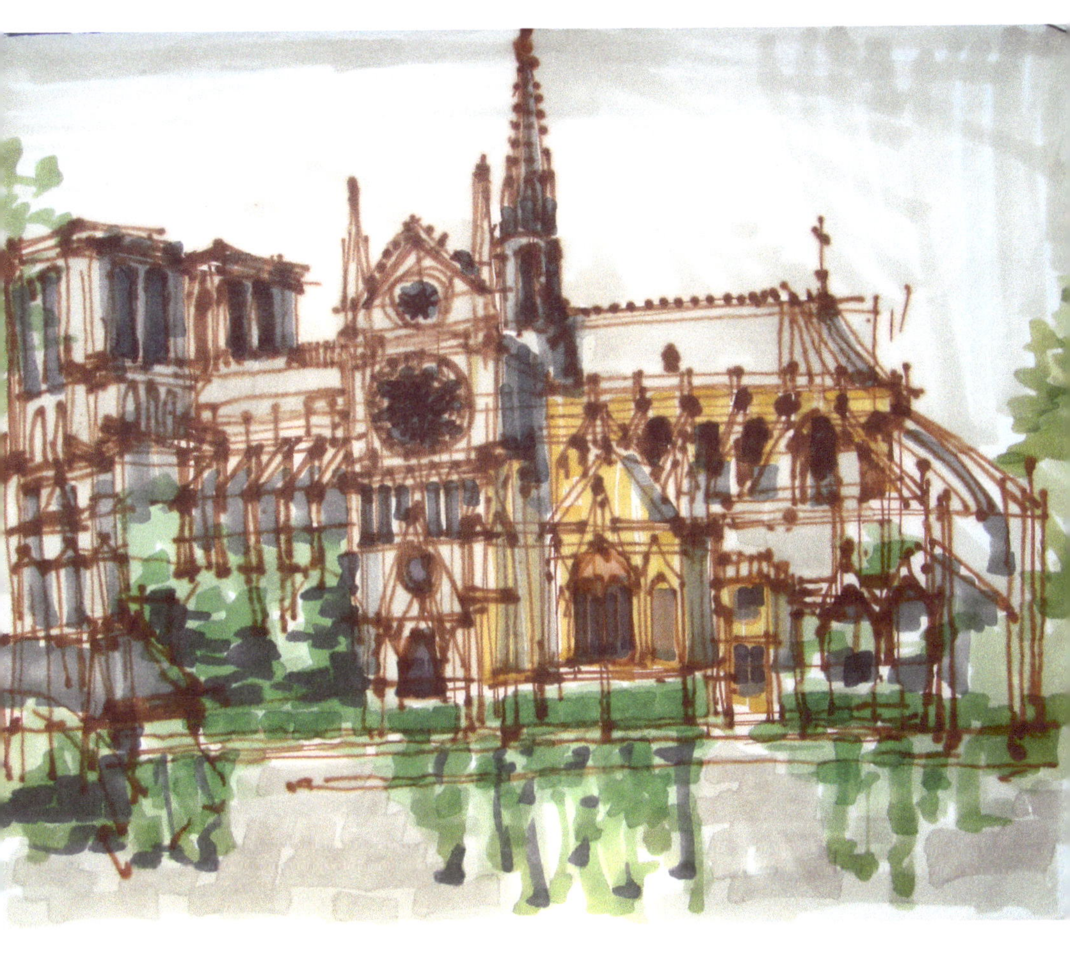

Loire River Valley, France

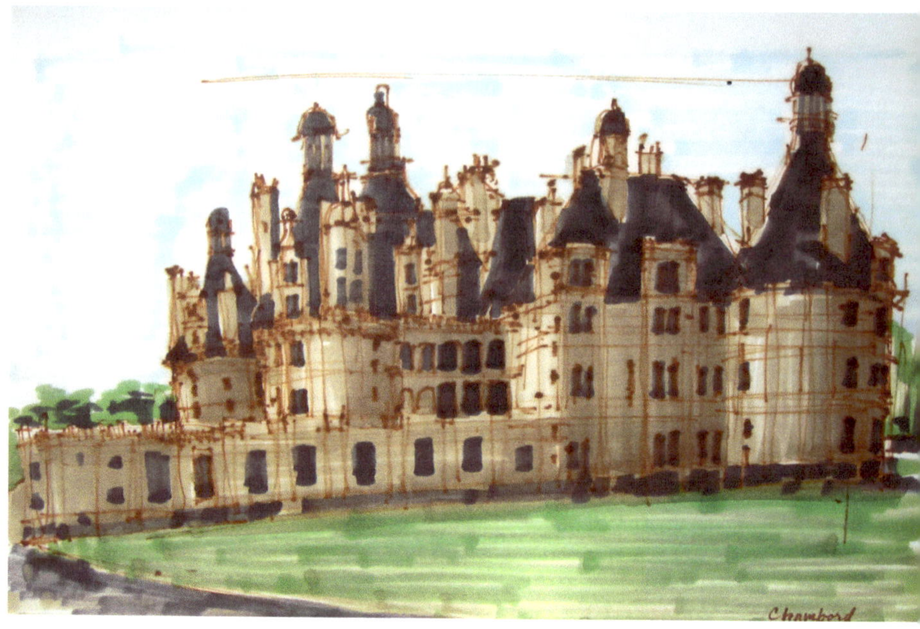

Clockwise from left: Chambord, Amboise, and Chaumont Castles

Along the Loire River Valley, the beautiful French countryside has many gorgeous and unique châteaux. Driving through France on the way to the city of Tours, you pass many wonderful castles and palaces. It's truly hard to resist stopping at each these castles and palaces to draw them. Since there were other travelers with me, I didn't want to take too much time sketching each castle but wanted to get the general feeling of proportion and size. You can see that the drawings are quick and sketchy and yet they capture the essence in the proportion of these buildings that have a history of many hundreds of years.

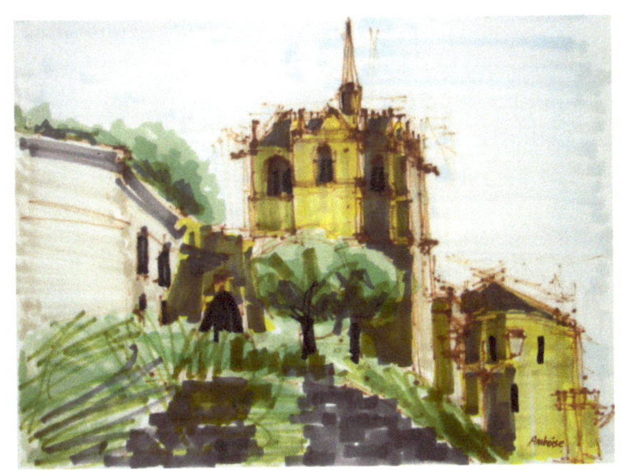

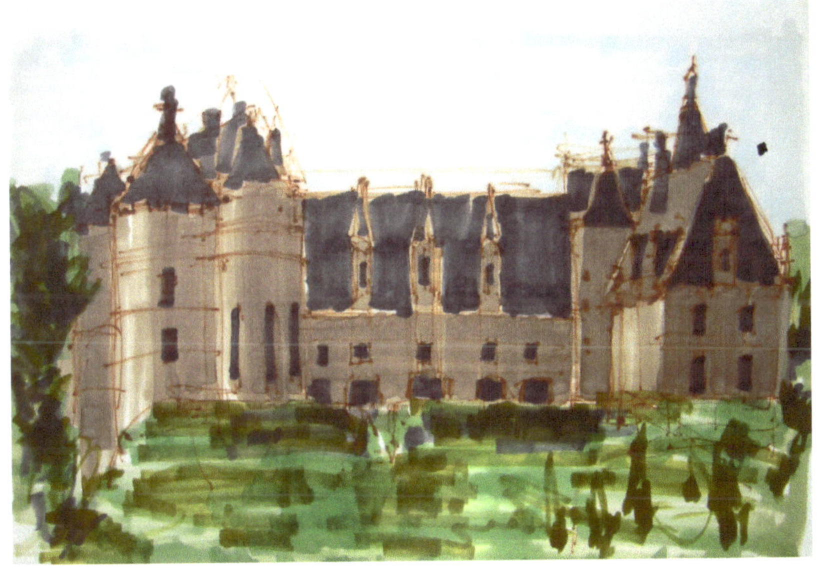

Sacre Coeur, a Roman Catholic Church and basilica, is a popular landmark located at the top of Montmartre, the highest point in Paris. It is very recognizable and architecturally unique, sometimes described as a free interpretation of Romano-Byzantine features. Tourists can go to the top of the dome and have a spectacular view of the city of Paris. It is also in a very crowded, tourist-filled area.

To find space to sketch, one must work his way around the many tourists and I was able to find a spot near the bottom of the long stairway leading to the church. I placed my drawing pad on a low wall there and spent some time studying the rich architectural detail of the church and basilica – it's stones, steeples, domes, windows and archways. Drawing a structure like this enables you to always remember those special architectural details that make the Sacré Coeur one of the world's most unique buildings.

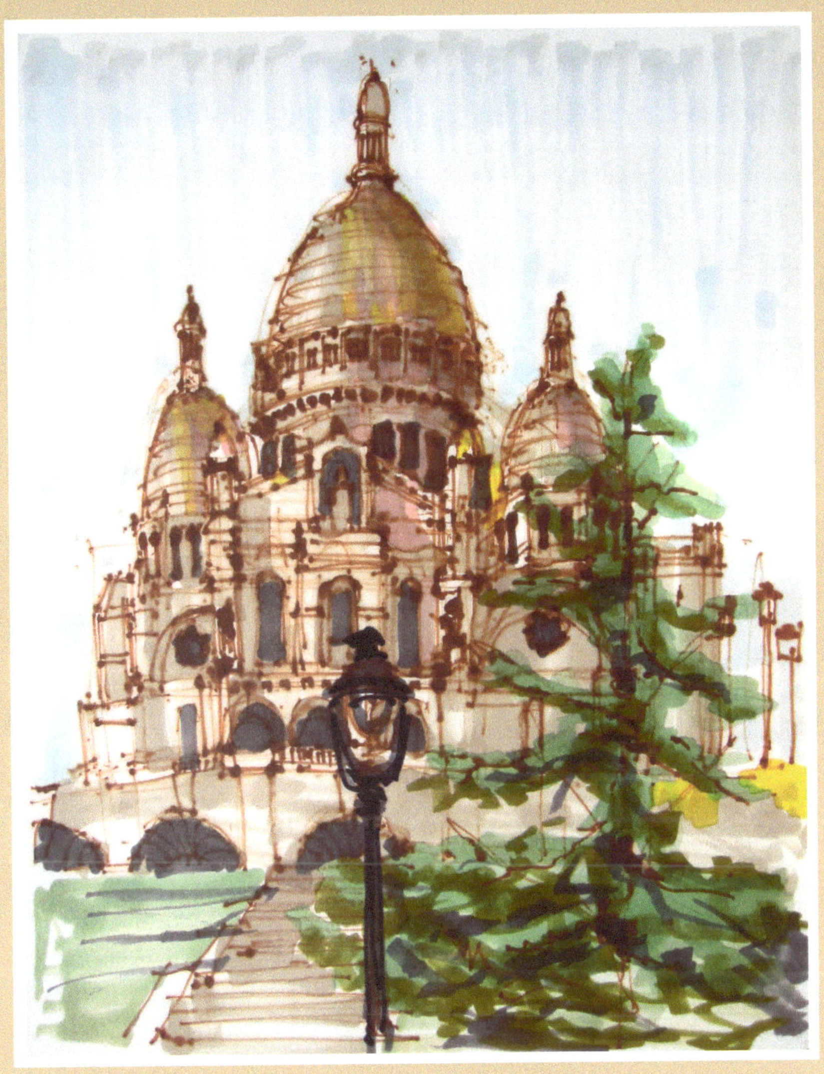

Sketching in Florence, Italy

Florence, Italy is a city that absolutely should not be missed. Everywhere you go there are sights to behold and you feel that there are so many places to capture as interesting drawings, which you will always remember. It's somewhat easy to get around the city of Florence, and you can cover a lot of territory by just walking with your drawing pad and finding interesting places to sketch and scenes that you will want to keep as fond memories.

When entering one of Florence's many archways, one of the very ornate buildings led my sight to this marvelous structure known as the Palazzo Vecchia. To me it reflected the combination of a fort, palace, and Italian campanile. The spacing of the elements and the proportion of the structure with its tiers and windows made an interesting building to sketch. Intrigued by the foreground archway, I used it to frame the structure,and add dimension.

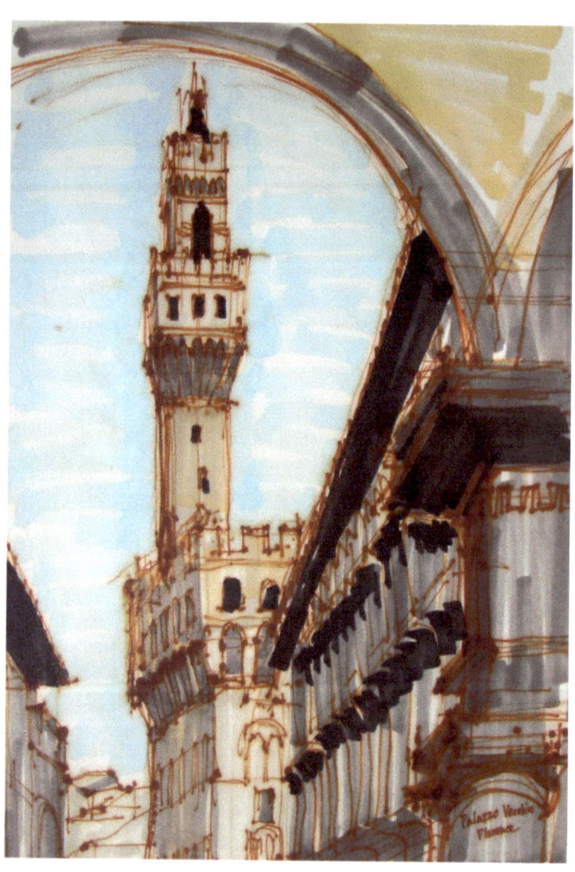

By taking the time to make this drawing, I will always recognize and remember the Palazzo Vecchia whenever I see a photograph representing this part of Florence.

Oaxaca, Mexico

The state of Oaxaca is in the southern part of Mexico bordering on the Pacific Ocean. Its main city, also named Oaxaca, is popular with tourists because of the city's areas of enclaves for rug making, painting, pottery, clothing, and many other crafts in which the people in that area excel. Jewelry making is also popular there and the prices for silver and gold are unusually reasonable in Oaxaca.

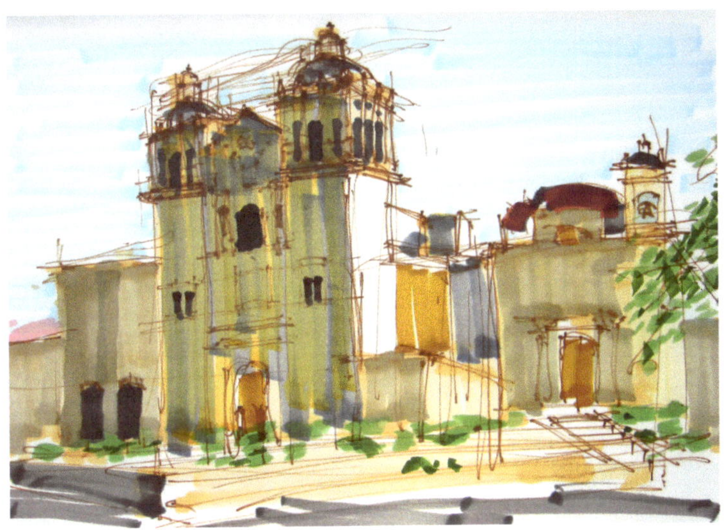

Within the city, there were some interesting places to sketch, and I found this church and the square around it fascinating, since it reminded me of so many Mexican churches I've seen in photographs. I studied the window treatments and the church proportions and, without taking much time, made the sketch.

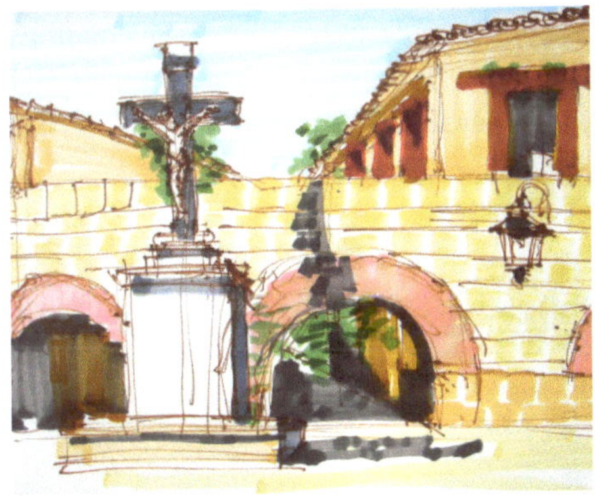

This Mexican courtyard caught my eye because of the severity of the structures – the combination of the crucifix, round archway, and windows. I sat on the ground in this courtyard to draw the pictural elements. Although it wasn't a remarkable scene, it was something that I can fondly remember.

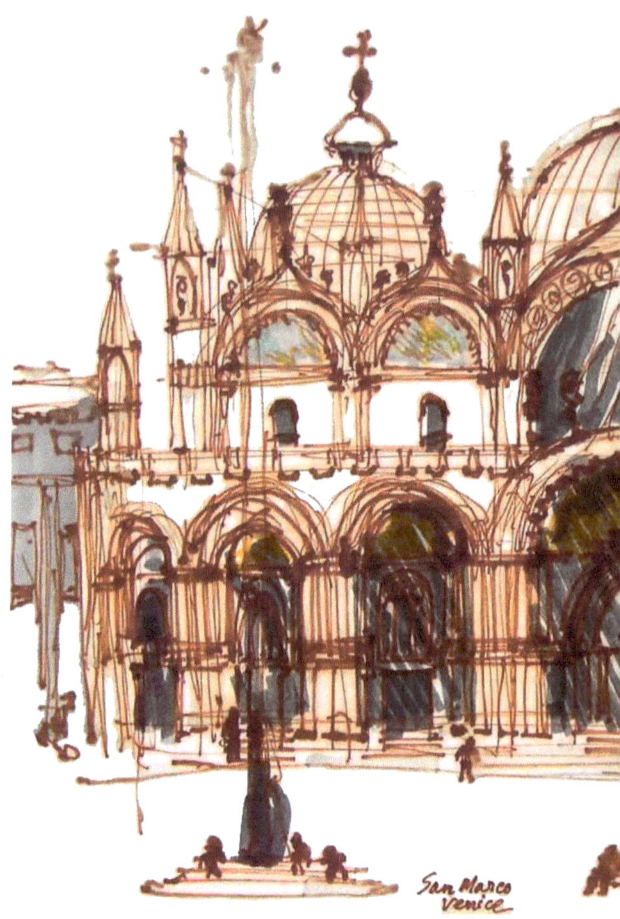

San Marco, Venice

Probably every tourist that goes to Venice, Italy visits Piazza San Marco. It is a large, open plaza area often filled with people and pigeons. The buildings are unique and very recognizable, especially St. Mark's Basilica (above). But yet, few people really know how those archways and Romanesque arches relate to each other and relate to all the other elements in this structure.

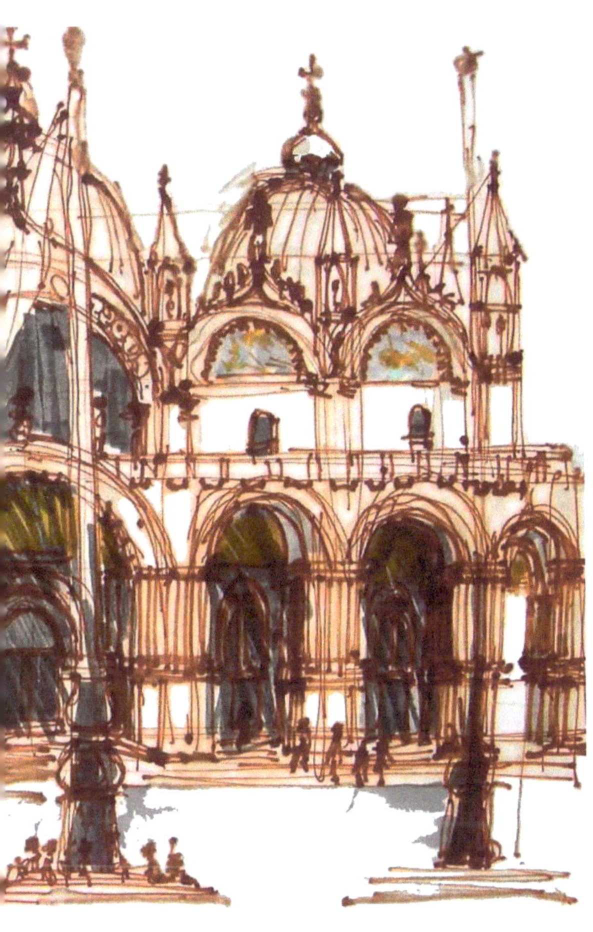

By making the drawing, I studied the details and can now remember the domes, the archways, the windows, the doorways, and all the architectural elements surrounding each of the steeples and domes. Although many photographs have been taken of the structure throughout the years, few photographers would take the opportunity to study all these architectural details the way somebody who draws the structure would. And I thank San Marco for being a place that I know and understand aesthetically and emotionally.

Sketching in Venice, Italy

In Venice this is affectionately known as "the Bridge of Sighs." Made of white limestone, you view it when you stand on a pedestrian bridge that crosses the Rio di Palazzo. Once again, I wanted to understand the architectural and window elements in the details that made this scene so beautiful, so I stood on the pedestrian bridge to make the drawing. It's a difficult place from which to draw, since the bridge is filled with tourists who take up most of the standing space. I found a spot near the bridge wall, placed my drawing pad on this wall and sketched – with a bit of discomfort – as quickly as I could, so that I could move away from the crowds as soon as possible. Once I started sketching, I found myself absorbed with the beauty of the archway and the details on the surrounding buildings, waterway, boats and pass-through. Capturing this in a drawing was a bit of a challenge, but worth it with the memories it holds.

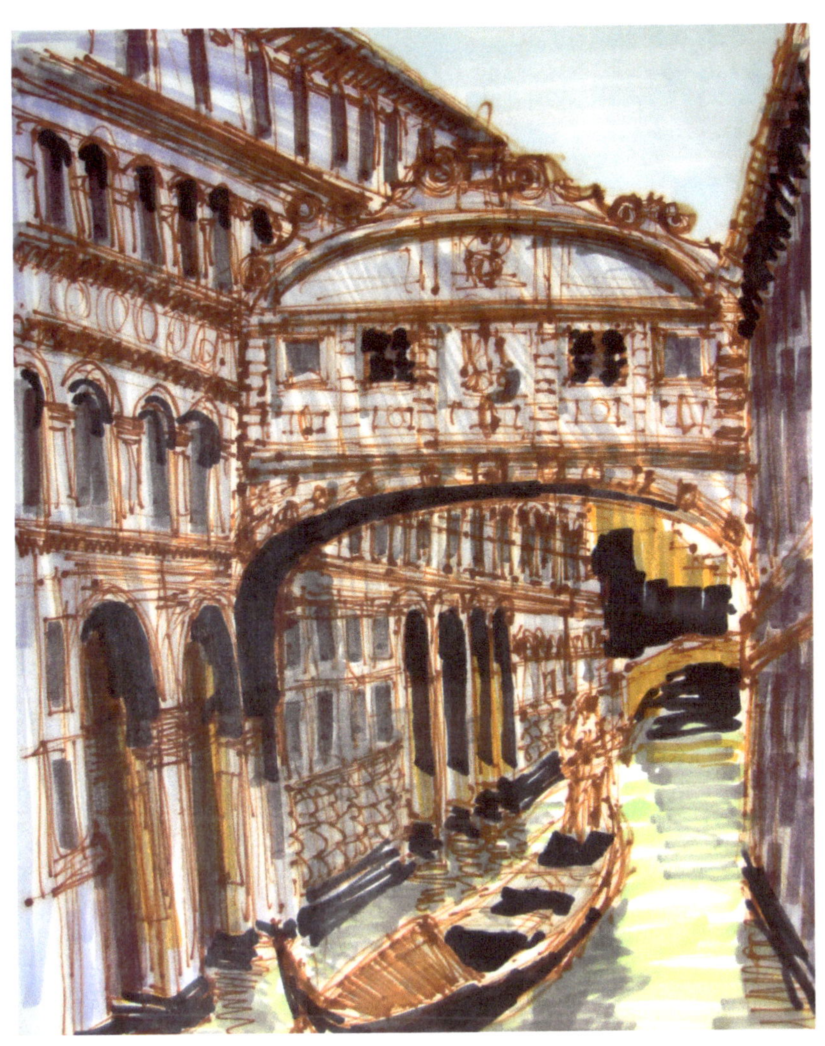

Venice, Italy

Since Venice is made up of waterways that are its actual streets, going from one section to another means you are constantly crossing bridges or taking a boat taxi along the water. During my stay in Venice it was delightful to take strolls and walk over these many bridges from which I could fully admire the scenery.

I stood on one of the bridges to capture and sketch this bridge called the Sotoportego de la Acque in Venice. As I was sketching there, a local family spent quite a bit of time watching me draw and I received compliments when the drawing was finished, especially from the children who were watching.

Seine River, Paris

Many say that the real essence of the city of Paris is captured by the Seine River. It flows through the heart of Paris and is the chief commercial waterway of the city. The Seine is surrounded by wonderful structures and many old bridge crossings. It is a treat to the eyes for all tourists and residents and adds to the beauty of Paris. The old buildings with their French Beaux-Arts architecture and the span of bridges made the sketch interesting for me, and in many ways, represent what Paris is all about. These are the scenes that encourage you to draw.

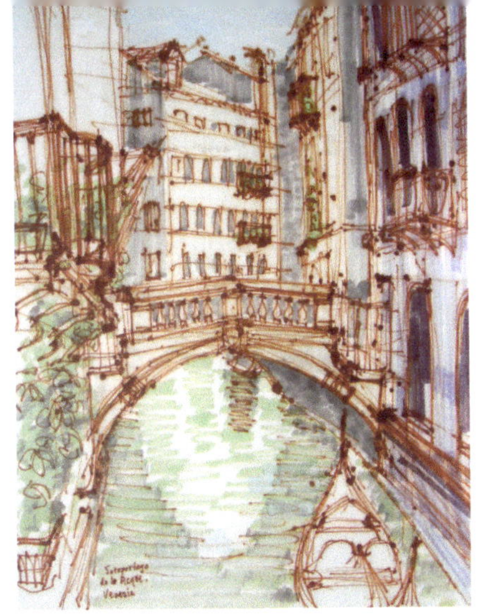

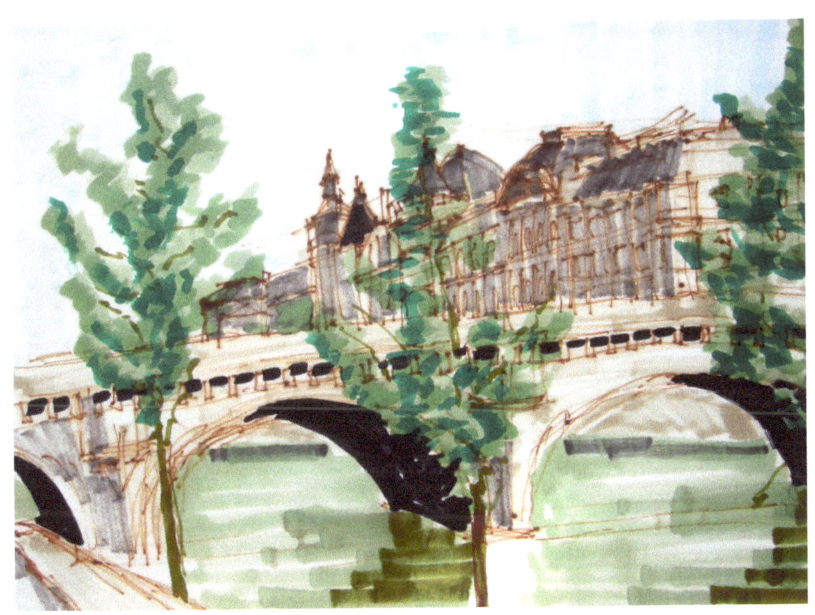

Kyoto, Japan

Having visited Japan and spending some time there, the city that I found most enchanting was Kyoto, about two hours on the bullet train from Tokyo. Kyoto is a charming old world city with many historic structures, palaces and shrines. Without a lot of time to spend in Kyoto, we tried to do as much touring as possible and took buses to various sites around the city. It is also a wonderful city just to walk around looking for new discoveries. Many streets are shopping streets with ancient specialty shops and markets.

Some say that Kyoto represents the best of early Japan and this is what makes it so fascinating for tourists. I read that there are over 1000 Buddhist temples in Kyoto. This site – called Kotano Tenmangu Shrine – was charming on both the inside and outside. I spent some time outside with my sketch pad on a table and did a sketch of the shrine. To me it reflected the Japanese architecture that I had always seen in the movies and the simplicity of forms within the architecture, including the symmetrical roof and the very simple window structures. In Japan it is evident that everything is examined carefully -- even the placement of the trees and the pruning of the trees -- to insure that all the elements work together in an aesthetic matter.

We took a bus trip out to the Kiyomizu-dera Temple, one of the main landmarks of the city. This ancient temple juts over a hillside and there are several other shrines surrounding the temple, attracting busloads of tourists. There are many steps to climb to inspect the ancient structure. The architecture is of the type that represents historic Japan – the combination of pagoda, roof and columns and the openness of the front entry.

Once again, sketching it is quite different from taking a photograph, since as an artist you have the opportunity to look closely at all the architectural elements, including the moldings, the decor and the pieces of the pagoda that make it unique. Although this drawing was made somewhat hastily, I still had the opportunity to study the proportions and the elements that make up this very interesting structure.

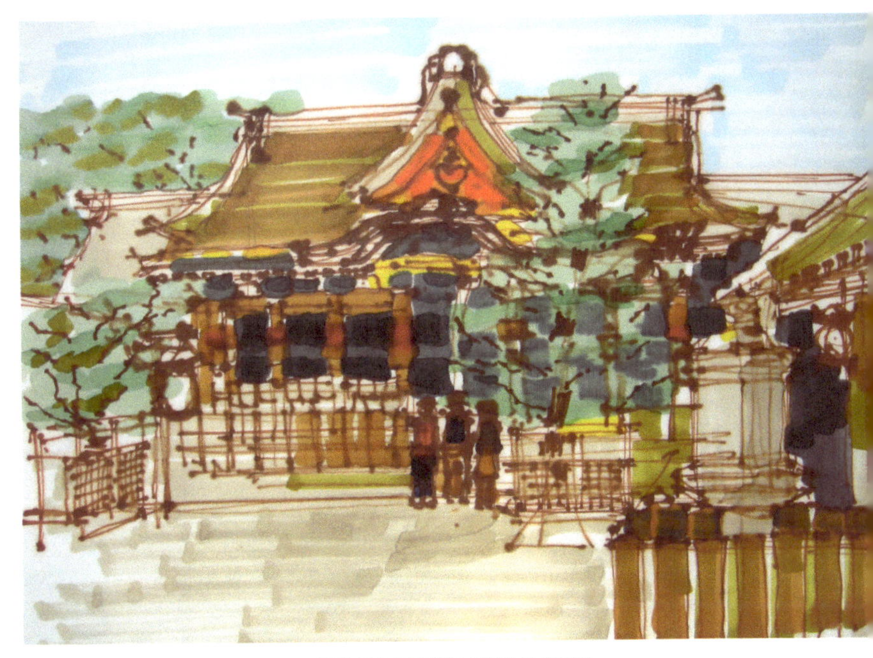

KOTANO TENMANGU SHRINE

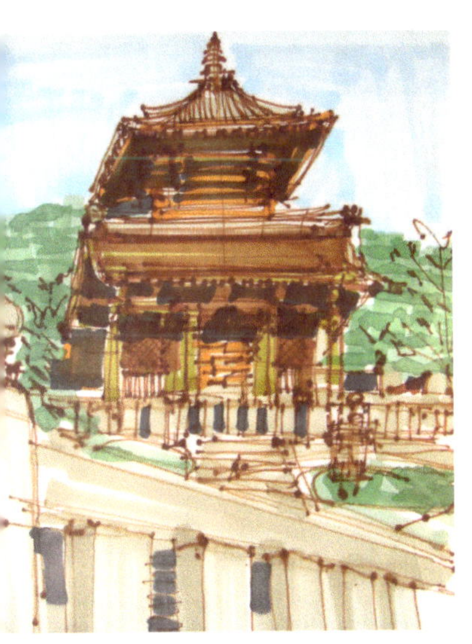

KIYOMIZU–DERA TEMPLE

Reproducing Your Art

You have created a sketchbook or multiple sketchbooks that you may want to keep for posterity. However, there are many ways to print copies from your original sketches that you can share with family and friends. You may also wish to sell some of the drawings on the market.

From the original sketches in your sketchbook, you can reproduce them, frame them, and then share them.

There are many options for reproducing your art, not only in its original size, but also in sizes that are smaller than the original or much larger. Some of the options for reproducing your sketches include:
Your home printer
Copy center or your local pharmacy
Online reproduction printmaker
Fine art printer
Printing on canvas

If you have a color printer at home that you use with your computer, you can take a photo of your sketch, and send the image to your home printer to print in the size that you prefer. If your home printer has a flatbed copy area, you can always place the sketchpad directly on the flatbed, either calibrate for the same size print or a larger print up to 8 x 10". If you do not have a home printer, you can do the same at a copy center such as Staples or FedEx. The copy centers have the advantage of directly printing on a flatbed copier that prints up to 11 x 17".

A copy center or your local pharmacy can also make large poster-prints for you, such as 14 x 17", 16 x 20" and larger. For prints that are not made directly from your sketchbook onto the flatbed copier, you will need to take a photo of your sketch and provide the image for the copy center or pharmacy.

There are also many commercial online printers that will make prints to any size that you wish from the image you provide for them. A good photo from your camera of your sketch will enable you to end up with a print or multiple prints in the size you designate. You can use your smartphone camera to photograph the image from your sketchbook.

Some online commercial printers specialize in art prints – printing on fine art papers. This is a good option for a truly high-quality print of a favorite drawing that you have made. This type of printing is more expensive than your local copy center, but you have your choice of different types of high quality art paper that they will provide for you. Many of these printers also will apply your sketch to canvas in any size, as long as you provide for them a good photo image of your drawing.

Determine the size

When you have decided the method you would like to use for reproducing your art, it will be important to arrive at the right size print for matting and framing. For cost purposes, a stock size frame is good to use, since custom size frames can be extremely expensive. Stock frames come in sizes such as 8 x 10, 11 x 14, 14 x 17, 16 x 20 and even larger. Anything larger than 8 x 10 is usually not appropriate for printing on your home printer.

iPad Sketches

I should mention at this time that any drawings you have done on the iPad can be treated in the same manner as I have described above. You even eliminate the step of photographing your drawing, since the iPad serves as a photographic medium and the iPad drawing can be shared via email, or printed in the various manners that I have described above.

How I make and frame prints

On the following pages, I will give you an example of how I reproduce my sketches and share the reproductions with friends, family and sometimes for sale.

I make my sketches on a sketchpad that is 11 x 14". Since copy centers such as FedEx and Staples have copy machines that accommodate 11 x 17" paper, I bring my sketchpad to the copy center. I place my 11 x 14" sketchpad on the flatbed copier.

In order to allow for space above and below the 11 inch dimension of the drawing, I adjust the copy machine to a 92% size, meaning that the print reproduction will be 92% of the size of the original.

I then make a single print to determine if the print being made is not too light or too dark. Sometimes I find that I need to set the printer a bit lighter, sometimes a bit darker in order to achieve an accurate reproduction of my sketch. It may take 2 or 3 single prints before the color is just right.

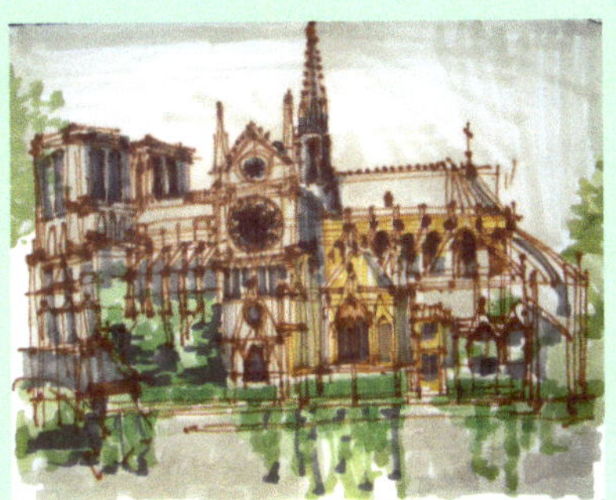

ORIGINAL PAGE FROM SKETCHPAD

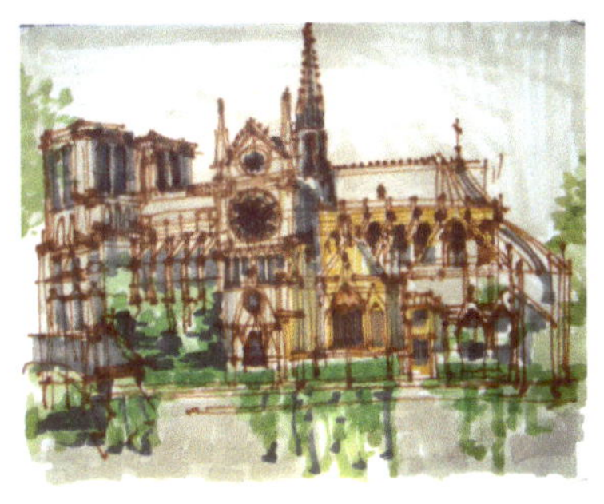

IMAGE PRINTED 92% SIZE ON WHITE PAPER

I usually ask at the front desk of the copy center for the heaviest white print paper that I can use in their copy machine and they will load up the copy machine with the heaviest paper they have available.

Having decided how many prints I want -- let's use 10 as a hypothetical figure – I set the copy machine to reproduce 10 copies from my original.

After the 10 prints are made in the 11 x 17" size, I cut down the 17 inch sides of the paper so that the final size is 11 x 14". Since I had designated the reproduction to be 92% of my original size, there is space around the sketch image for numbering the print and for my signature. Also, there is space for either a matte, frame, or both.

I sign and number each of the reproduction prints. I like to give the prints a name so that the image is recognizable to anyone who sees the print. On the bottom of the paper is the name of the print, the number of prints that I have made, and my signature. It's important to number each of your prints, so that the recipient understands that it is from a series of prints that you are providing, and not the original. This gives the print the meaning of "Limited Edition."

Since 11 x 14" is a standard size, any art supply store will have mattes in various colors that accommodate 11 x 14" prints. This is also true for 5 x 7", 8 x 10", 14 x 17", and sometimes even larger.

The 11 x 14" matte usually has an outside dimension of 16 x 20", which is a standard stock size for a frame. So I am able to use a standard size matte, in a color that complements the image, and a standard stock size frame that complements the matte and the print.

This same method of reproduction, matting and framing can apply to any size with which you like to work.

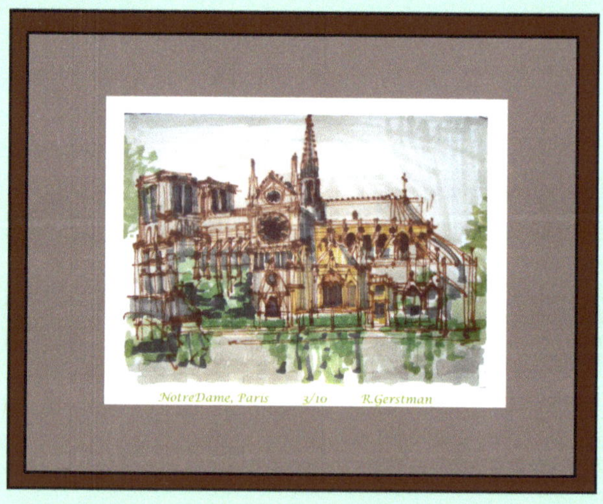

SIGNED AND NUMBERED LIMITED–EDITION PRINT, MATTED AND FRAMED

With iPad sketches, I can do the same with one main difference: the first step is to print the iPad sketch on my home printer in an 8 x 10" size. From that 8 x 10" print, I go to the copy center and, using the method that I described two pages earlier, convert the 8 x 10" prints into reproductive hardcopies of 11 x 14". I also sign and number the iPad prints as I have done with the print shown on the previous page..

I do enjoy sharing my limited edition prints with friends, family and also with people who wish to buy them. The next step, after reproducing, signing, matting and framing is the shipping.

SHIPPING YOUR ART

For shipping the prints, your best option is to use a shipping center such as FedEx or UPS. They will pack your framed print and ship it for you.

Before I bring it to the shipping store, I believe it is important to protect the frame from possible breakage. Most stock size frames come with glass. Shipping glass is risky and I know from experience that not all frames -- even when packed well -- arrive without glass breakage. So I substitute clear plastic for the glass from the stock size frame. Most hardware stores will cut clear plastic to the size that you need. I request the 16 x 20" plastic and replace the glass in the stock frame with this new piece of clear plastic. So there is never a worry that there will be a problem with shipping.

There are more options for reproducing your art than can be imagined. Some of the online reproduction stores not only reproduce on various materials, but also mount and even laminate your print if you wish.

Original marker sketches and water color sketches will start to fade when exposed to sunlight for long periods. The good thing is that you have been able to enjoy making the sketches and now you are able to share the memories of your travels with relatives and friends who can also enjoy and hang the limited edition treasures on their walls!